GRASSROOTS

GRASSROOTS
THE WRITER'S WORKBOOK

Susan Fawcett   **Alvin Sandberg**

Bronx Community College

HOUGHTON MIFFLIN COMPANY   **BOSTON**

Atlanta   Dallas   Geneva, Illinois
Hopewell, New Jersey   Palo Alto   London

Printed in the United States of America

Library of Congress Catalog Card Number: 75-37475
ISBN: 0-395-24063-8

CONTENTS

PREFACE

There will always be students who groan at the thought of "English class" or "compositions." Some of these students have simply never discovered that writing can be a source of fun and power. Others, unfortunately, have no choice but to groan since they find themselves enrolled in college yet lacking those basic writing skills necessary to success in college and in many careers. Often these students are mature, articulate, perhaps potentially fine writers, but when it comes to grammar . . . . Well, somewhere along the line they never learned their "English."

This book was designed especially for such students. The name *Grassroots* reflects our attempt to be as down to earth and as helpful as possible. As writing teachers at a large community college, we found that many grammar books just did not teach anything; usually they contained too many rules and too few practical exercises. Thus, we began to create worksheets in direct response to the writing needs of our students. Our approach seemed to help students learn English, and we decided to make this book.

Since we assume that people learn to write by writing, our aim has been to include as many practice sections and as little formal explanation as possible. A student may do grammar drills faithfully, then make the same old errors when he or she writes a theme. So, we have varied the exercises and always come back to the actual process of writing.

Grassroots is adaptable to almost any teaching/learning situation—classroom, tutorial, self-teaching. Each chapter is a self-contained lesson. A student needing work in just two or three areas—say *-ed* verbs and the apostrophe—can go straight to the chapters tailored to his or her needs. The sequence of chapters may be individualized, or the book may be taught from start to finish.

Special thanks go to Dorie and Dick, Joan and Jean for their encouragement and patience throughout this project, to Marna for help and enthusiasm, to Carole for typing. We are grateful to our colleagues for their suggestions, to Evelyn, Hannah, and Miriam for their kind assistance, and to our students—who inspired us to write this book.

Susan Fawcett   Alvin Sandberg

1
GETTING STARTED

Often the most difficult part of writing a composition is *beginning*—just getting yourself and your ideas together enough to write. This chapter will show you some steps you can take before you begin to write so that when you are finished you have said exactly what you wanted to say. Here are five basic steps you should take *before you write*.

> **STEP ONE:**   Limiting
> **STEP TWO:**   Brainstorming
> **STEP THREE:**   Eliminating
> **STEP FOUR:**   Grouping
> **STEP FIVE:**   Arranging

These steps will be explained one at a time.

STEP ONE: Limiting

Very often an instructor will assign a topic that may seem too broad. What he or she wants is for you to deal with only one aspect of that subject without getting lost and jumping from one idea to another.

Keep in mind that for most topics you might write many pages but that your task is usually to write a page or two. Therefore, you must *limit*—cut your topic down to size and pick one area that you want to work on.

Example:

TOPIC:	LIMITATION:	FURTHER LIMITATION:
Racial Problems	Prejudice in Housing	Poor Sanitation Services in the Ghetto

Racial Problems would easily fill a hundred books (and has), but *Prejudice in Housing* is one limited aspect of *Racial Problems* to write one theme about. Of course, *Prejudice in Housing* is still a large topic, and you might want to further limit the topic to *Poor Sanitation Services in the Ghetto.*

How much you limit is up to you, but always try to make your topic as narrow and confined as possible. Remember: very often, the most specific and detailed writing is the best.

Practice

Here are some possible theme topics. How would you limit each of them?

Topic:	**Limitation:**
1. Women	1. _____
2. Politics	2. _____
3. My First Reaction to College	3. _____
4. Hobbies	4. _____
5. My Next Vacation	5. _____
6. How Cities Could Be Improved	6. _____
7. A Good Career	7. _____
8. An Autobiography	8. _____

Now, see if you can limit still more. How would you further limit each possible topic above? Write the second limitation here:

Further Limitation:

1. _____

2. _____

3. _____

4. _____

5. _____

6. _____

7. _____

8. _____

STEP TWO: Brainstorming

Once you have an idea of what limited area your paper will cover, it is time to *brainstorm*: that is, to write down anything and everything you can think of that pertains to your limited topic.

At times, an idea will occur to you that does not really fit into the topic. That's okay. For now, just keep jotting down ideas. Don't stop. Keep moving.

Practice

Pick one topic that interests you (possibly one from the list) and limit it. Write your topic and limitation here:

Topic: _____ **Limitation:** _____

Now, brainstorm! Just write anything that comes to you about your limited topic. Don't worry about writing a theme. Just get ideas down on paper! Everything!

Brainstorm:

1.

2.

3.

4.

5.

6.

7.

8.

9.

10.

11.

12.

13.

14.

15. and more . . .

STEP THREE: Eliminating

This is the easiest step, since all you have to do is drop the ideas that don't fit in and don't belong to your limited topic. Here is an example of brainstorming based on one of the topics listed previously, *My First Reaction to College*. Suppose this topic has already been limited to one reaction—*confusion*. Which ideas below develop the new limited topic, *Confusion Was My First Reaction to College*? Which ideas would you drop? Why?

- couldn't find class
- food too expensive
- campus too large
- felt like a small fish in a big pond
- guards weren't helpful
- teachers weren't sure of their sections
- some buildings are old and have peeling paint on the walls
- I couldn't find my rooms
- some offices were hard to find
- got lost on the train
- didn't know whom to ask for help

Practice

Now go back to your own brainstorming list; eliminate ideas that do not develop the topic as you have limited it.

Remember, you should be able to give good reasons for keeping or dropping an idea.

STEP FOUR: Grouping

After you have eliminated all the ideas that do not belong to your theme, it's time to *group* your thoughts together; group together ideas that have something in common, that are related or alike in some way. Here are the ideas of *My First Reaction to College* grouped together in one possible combination:

- guards weren't helpful
- I couldn't find my rooms
- teachers weren't sure of their sections

- I felt like a small fish in a big pond
- campus too large

- some offices were hard to find
- didn't know whom to ask for help

How are the ideas in each group above related? Keep in mind that there is more than one way to group ideas. As *you* group your own brainstorming, think of what *you* want to say; then group ideas according to what *your point is*.

Practice

Group your own ideas here:

STEP FIVE: Arranging

This step is closely related to grouping. After you have placed your thoughts into two, three, four, or more groups, *arrange the groups* into some kind of logical sequence or order. Ask yourself these questions:

- Which group of ideas should come first in the paper? Why?
- Which group should follow? Why?
- What's next? Why?
- Which group of ideas should be last? Why?

Practice

Arrange your grouped ideas from step four into some logical order. Justify your sequence.

Now that you have *limited, brainstormed, eliminated, grouped* and *arranged*—it's time to write your theme.

Let's go!

2
BEGINNING AND ENDING SENTENCES

There is only one way to begin a sentence—*a capital letter*.

There are three ways to end a sentence—*a period*, **an** *exclamation point*, **or** **a** *question mark*.

PERIOD   .

○ Use a *period* at the end of a sentence that makes a statement.

Example: I went to the same movie eight times this week.

EXCLAMATION POINT   !

○ Use an *exclamation point* at the end of a sentence that commands or expresses a strong emotion.

Example: Get out!
              Wow!

(Use the exclamation point sparingly.)

QUESTION MARK   ?

○ Use a *question mark* at the end of a sentence that asks a question.

Example: Where are you going?

Practice 1

Begin and end these sentences properly.

1. how are you feeling
2. please sit down immediately
3. the students gave the instructor a gift
4. did the instructor give the students a present
5. too much soda rots your teeth
6. get out of there right now
7. he has often wondered how a question mark is used
8. autumn in this part of the country is colorful
9. where are my beige sneakers
10. writing is one way to learn about yourself

Practice 2

Write 5 sentences ending with a period, 5 ending with a question mark and 5 ending with an exclamation point. Make sure that you begin the sentences correctly.

1. _____

2. _____

3. _____

4. _____

5. _____

6. _____

7. _____

8. _____

9. _____

10. _____

11. _____

11. _____

12. _____

13. _____

14. _____

15. _____

3
SUBJECTS AND VERBS

PART A: Defining and Spotting the Subject
PART B: Singular and Plural Subjects
PART C: Defining and Spotting Action Verbs
PART D: Defining and Spotting Linking Verbs
PART E: Spotting Verbs of More than One Word
PART F: Review of Subjects and Verbs

PART A: Defining and Spotting the Subject
(who or what words)

(1) _____ jumped over the black Buick, scaled the building and finally reached the roof.

(2) _____ needs a new coat of paint.

These sentences might be very interesting in terms of what they could say. But as they stand, they are incomplete because of what they don't say.

- In sentence (1), *who* "jumped," "scaled" and "reached"? Batman, Shaft, Santa Claus, the English teacher?
- Depending on *who* did the action—jumping, scaling, or reaching—the sentence can be silly, exciting, or dumb.
- What is missing is the *who* word.
- In sentence (2), would it matter if you were talking about the *car* or the *house* or the *kitchen?*
- Obviously, *what* needs a new coat of paint is vital to the sentence.
- What is missing is the *what* word.

Practice   1

In all of these sentences, the **who** or **what** word has been omitted. Fill in your own **who** or **what** word to make the sentence complete.

1. _____ owns a black car.

2. On Thursday, _____ went to watch the women's basketball game.

3. The _____ looked good standing in the corner, but my _____ moved it back to the attic.

4. _____ helps build strong bodies and good minds.

5. The _____ brought me $100 at the auction.

6. The pink _____ jumped through the hoop as the _____ looked on and applauded.

7. My _____ appears older than it really is.

8. _____ makes good eating on a hot summer day.

9. The _____ played "Going Uptown" 20 times, and the _____ couldn't stop dancing.

10. Setting up for the game, _____ put the chairs in a circle.

11. If _____ does his homework, _____ will let him go to the game.

12. The _____ crashed into the pole.

13. My great grandfather's _____ has been passed on from generation to generation.

14. Because of poor lighting, _____ spilled milk on the rug.

15. Her _____ fell to the floor and smashed.

16. _____ is the most beautiful building on the campus, but I prefer having my classes in the auditorium.

17. _____ hoped that her _____ would arrive on time.

18. These _____ are really dull.

19. My _____ wanted to see *A Raisin in the Sun,* but _____ had seen it already.

20. Every Tuesday _____ goes to the library to research his term paper.

In order for a sentence to be complete, it must contain a *who* or *what* word.

The *who* or *what* word is called the subject.

The subject tells you *who* or *what* does something or exists in a certain way.

Practice   2

Circle the *subject* in these sentences. The *subject* is the **who** or **what** word.

1. The girl kissed her best friend.
2. A large green tree grew near the lake.
3. By 4:00 a.m., the fire had spread to the whole block.
4. A gang robbed my grocery store.
5. On Thursdays, my niece always goes to the movies.
6. My father's car rolled down the hill and hit a wall.
7. Walking down the street, the young woman spotted her parents on a bus.
8. The students wrote their term papers over the Christmas holiday.
9. Macy's is having a fantastic sale on winter coats.
10. That dirty old dog sat in my favorite chair.
11. Tomatoes grow rapidly in warm weather.
12. He took the large dog for a walk around the park.
13. I saw a yellow cigarette case near the bed.
14. All day the heavy rain drenched the street.
15. The book provided many good pictures of the African plains.

Practice   3

Now that you have had practice in filling subjects in blank spaces and circling subjects, these exercises are a final check on whether you completely understand subjects.

In these sentences, the subject has been omitted, and you must find out where it would fit and fill one in. Put in a **who** or **what** word (subject) that makes sense. (You may have to fill in more than one subject in a sentence.)

Example: Ran down the street.
            My friend ran down the street.

1. Stopped at the grocery and bought some cupcakes.

   _____

2. Always goes to the library after he visits his parents in Brooklyn.

   _____

3. On Monday had to appear at the Dean's Office to receive her award.

   _____

4. All day long, my slept curled up in the corner.

    _____

5. Are never on time, but like them anyway.

    _____

6. Because of the party upstairs, fell off the shelf and broke.

    _____

7. If want to learn to play guitar, have to practice.

    _____

8. At the dance, spent three hours doing the cha-cha until couldn't move any longer.

    _____

PART B: Singular and Plural Subjects

Now that you are able to spot subjects fairly easily, you are ready for additional work on them.

---

(1) The boy jogged around the park.

○ The subject of the sentence is *the boy*.
○ Since *the boy* is one person, the subject is *singular*.

Singular means only one of something.

---

(2) The boy and his instructor jogged around the park.

○ The subject of the sentence is *the boy and his instructor*.
○ Since *the boy and his instructor* are more than one person, the subject is *plural*.

Plural means more than one of something.

Practice   1

Here is a list of possible subjects of sentences. If the subject is **singular,** put a check in the **singular** column; if the subject is **plural,** put a check in the **plural** column.

Example:	(one) singular	(more than one) plural
a boy	✓	
the pencils		✓
students		✓

Possible Subjects	(one) singular	(more than one) plural
1. my parents	_____	_____
2. a grey Buick	_____	_____
3. three green ties	_____	_____
4. a shirt and a blouse	_____	_____
5. she	_____	_____
6. they	_____	_____
7. I	_____	_____
8. their packages	_____	_____
9. children	_____	_____
10. an uncle and an aunt	_____	_____
11. apple pie	_____	_____
12. apple pies	_____	_____
13. he	_____	_____
14. we	_____	_____
15. a book	_____	_____
16. people	_____	_____
17. her man	_____	_____
18. flowers	_____	_____
19. women	_____	_____
20. their trophy	_____	_____
21. a pen and a pencil	_____	_____
22. her secretary	_____	_____
23. dishes	_____	_____
24. yellow hat	_____	_____
25. a saxophone and the trumpet	_____	_____

Practice 2

Circle the subjects in these sentences. In the blank at the right of the sentence, write an **S** if the subject is **Singular;** write **P** if the subject is **Plural.**

1. His mother and father came to visit him.   _____

2. His mother came to visit him.   _____

3. These fish tanks are beautiful.   _____

4. My textbook costs $8.00.   _____

5. I love apple pie for dessert.   ———

6. In the afternoon, we left for the football game.   ———

7. The baby ate sloppily.   ———

8. His books and mine are missing.   ———

9. His book and mine are missing.   ———

10. After the party, the dancers went home.   ———

11. I am so tired!   ———

12. She is very fond of her instructor.   ———

13. The chairman called the meeting to order.   ———

14. Cigarettes are bad for your health.   ———

15. Those lamps will look great in my apartment.   ———

16. The couch and the bookcase are in bad shape.   ———

17. By Thursday, all the classes were closed.   ———

18. Will he arrive on time?   ———

19. The man and the woman walked hand in hand.   ———

20. Susan is my best friend.   ———

21. They play basketball together.   ———

22. The students' papers were excellent.   ———

23. Their television set works badly.   ———

24. Dick seems to be a terrific guy.   ———

25. My typewriter and my radio need repairs.   ———

PART C: Defining and Spotting Action Verbs (do words)

> (1) Robert _____ his mother on the cheek and _____ his dog on the back.
>
> (2) The delicious fruit _____ in the field.

These sentences tell you *who* or *what* the subject is—"Robert" and the "delicious fruit"—but you don't know what the subject *does*.

○ In sentence (1), what does Robert *do*? What action does he perform?

○ Here are some possible choices for the *do words—pats, slaps, licks, kisses, taps, scratches,* or *strokes.*

○ All these *do words* (or action verbs) fit into the blank spaces in sentence (1), but the sentence changes depending on which *do words* are put in.

○ In sentence (2), what does the fruit *do*?

○ Does it *grow, rot, stink,* or *glow*?

○ Depending on which *do word* you fill in, the sentence changes its meaning.

In order for a sentence to be complete, it must have a *verb*.

One kind of *verb* is a *do word*, a word that shows action.

Practice   1

Fill in an action *verb* (a **do word**) in the blank space.

1. My dog always _____ on my father's bed.

2. The star quarterback just _____.

3. At 3:00, she _____ into the freezing lake.

4. When he _____ her, she _____ him.

5. The large man _____ the small boy.

6. The rock band _____ and the sweating crowd _____.

7. Please _____ your homework.

8. After they _____ the cabinets, the carpenters _____ their tools.

9. He never _____, but I do.

10. After the students _____ the test, the professor _____.

Practice   2

Circle the action verb (the **do word**) in these sentences. Some sentences contain more than one action *verb*.

1. The chubby baby drank a full bottle of milk.
2. Four thieves drove away with my new Lincoln.
3. His professor never marks themes during vacation.
4. A lovely woman sold fruit under the palm trees.
5. At the first sign of a cold, take a glass of orange juice.
6. Near dawn, the huge eagle circled its nest.
7. The slippery plate smashed against the stone floor.

8. My cousin ran to his best friend's house on 112th street.
9. On the first pitch, the lead-off man slammed a home-run into the bleachers.
10. Wow, he grew six inches in six months!
11. After he did his homework, Bill went to the park.
12. The students wanted the new instructor, but her classes closed early in registration.
13. These books bored me, but they fascinated everyone else.
14. In the winter, I stay in the house all day.
15. He won the court case because the lawyers fought very hard.

PART D: Defining and Spotting Linking Verbs

The verbs you have been examining so far all described some kind of action. But there is another kind of verb that you will have to learn to recognize.

> (1)   Wolfman Jack sometimes seems a little strange.

○ The subject is Wolfman Jack.
○ But there is no action verb (*do word*) in the sentence.
○ However, *seems* links the subject, *Wolfman Jack,* with the descriptive words, *a little strange.*

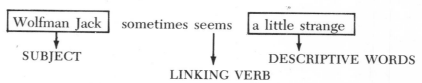

> (2)   They are pilots for the government.

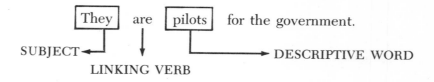

In order for a sentence to be complete, it must contain a *verb*.

One kind of *verb* is a *linking word,* a word that links the subject with a descriptive word in the sentence.

Practice   1

The subjects and descriptive words are blocked. Circle the linking verb.

1. | His cousin | appeared | unhappy | yesterday afternoon.

2. [They] felt [secure] about the final.

3. In the afternoon, [he] became [angry] when it rained.

4. [She] is [the best player] on the volleyball team.

5. [The rain] is [wet and cold] in the winter.

Practice 2

Circle the linking verbs in these sentences; underline the subject and the descriptive word. Note that the most common linking verb is *to be* (am, is, are, was, were).

1. My uncle was fat for ten years.
2. In the afternoon, the sky grew cloudy.
3. They were happy all their lives.
4. Dogs always feel frisky after a bath.
5. These houses appeared too dirty for human habitation.
6. Raphael is very studious.
7. She looks tired after the four hour chemistry laboratory.
8. Everyone seems relieved at the end of the semester.
9. Frankly, I am sorry for him.

Practice 3

In these sentences, the linking verb has been left out. Choose a linking verb from the list on the right and fit it in the correct spot in the sentence.

Example: I the teacher of the Shakespeare class.
            I *was* the teacher of the Shakespeare class.

1. He my best friend for many years.
2. When they received their grades, they happy.
3. The child ill after eating so many green apples.
4. Travelers often tired after long journeys. *appear*
5. The books filthy from all the ink spilled on them.
6. The salad to be a bit spicy for her taste.
7. My uncle an easy touch for a loan.
8. She beautiful every day.

were
seemed
are
appear
is
was
looks
looked
became
appeared

PART E: Spotting Verbs of More than One Word

All of the verbs you have dealt with so far have been single words—*look, walked, saw, are, were,* etc. But many verbs consist of more than one word.

---

(1)   He <u>is leaving</u> for school now.

○ The subject is *he*.
○ What is *he* doing?
○ He *is leaving*.
○ *Leaving* is the *main verb*.
○ *Is* is the *helping (or auxiliary) verb; is* helps *leaving*.

---

(2)   Robert has been there often.

○ The subject is *Robert*.
○ *Has been* is the *verb*.
○ *Been* is the *main verb*.
○ *Has* is the *helping (or auxiliary) verb; has* helps *been*.

---

(3)   I <u>would</u> have <u>gone</u> later.

○ What is the subject? _____ (fill in)

○ What is the main verb? _____ (fill in)

○ What are the helping verbs? _____ _____ (fill in)

Practice   1

The number of blanks to the right of each sentence tells you how many words make up the *verb*. Fill in the complete verb in these blanks and circle the main verb.

Example: He has been studying for a long time.   <u>has</u>   <u>been</u>   (studying)

1. I will go very soon. <u>will</u> <u>go</u>

2. My friend has seen this film before. <u>has</u> <u>seen</u>

3. The student should have finished the paper by now. <u>should</u> <u>have</u> <u>finished.</u>

4. Shall I bake a cake? _____ _____

5. They are leaving at 4:00. _____ _____.

6. They have been starving for a cold drink. _____

_____ _____

7. Are you reading the homework? _____ _____

8. That dog could have done anything. _could_ _have_ _don_

9. You really must clean this house. _mut_ _clean_

10. You should have completed the game on Sunday. _should_ _have_ _completed_

11. Yes, he does write beautiful poetry. _____ _____

12. They have never been to the circus before. _____ _____

13. He has looked tired every day this week. _____ _____

14. The janitor had seemed happy with the new elevator. _had_ _seemed_

15. She will have painted the whole apartment by now. _will_ _have_ _painted_

Practice 2

Now try these sentences without the help of the blank spaces. Circle the main verb and underline the helping or auxiliary verb(s).

1. Will you go to the dentist with me?
2. They had made a serious error.
3. He has seemed happy every day this week.
4. The children may play for an hour.
5. Instructors should always help their students.
6. In another ten minutes, I will have been waiting for four hours.
7. My guitar has been out of tune for weeks.
8. Have you repaired that flat tire?
9. You should have repaired it last week.
10. They were hoping for straight A's this semester.
11. He has never played *Monopoly* before.
12. Can you polish the mirrors for the party?
13. Her furniture has seen better days.
14. These flowers are wilting.
15. They could have tried harder.

PART F: Review of Subjects and Verbs

Circle the complete subject and underline the complete verb in these sentences. If you have a great deal of difficulty with this review, it may be best for you to reread the entire lesson.

1. The thirsty man gulped the ice cream soda.
2. My cousin and her friend came to the party late.

3. Her father and mother have been lawyers for years.
4. Robert and I left together.
5. The lineman smashed through the opposing team's defense.
6. The yellow submarine was parked in front of the gas station.
7. You should have swallowed the cough syrup quickly.
8. They have been my best friends for a long time.
9. Should I leave now?
10. Will he do his homework on time?
11. The judge could have sentenced the pusher to life.
12. We must help his little brother with mathematics.
13. The lamp has been burning all afternoon.
14. The shoes and the shirt seem too tight for him.
15. She will have eaten the cake by 3:00.
16. They have always written their papers on time.
17. My Persian cat has been crying for food for hours.
18. Are you going to the movies later?
19. She may try for a scholarship for medical school.
20. He and she are together all the time.
21. These books and those papers are missing.
22. Will you go to the dentist's office with me?
23. Rooms 212 and 213 have been empty all day.
24. You must leave the room immediately.
25. Those grammar exercises have been helpful.

THE WHOLE SENTENCE (Avoiding Fragments)

PART A: Writing Sentences with <u>Subjects and Verbs</u>
PART B: Writing Sentences with **Complete Verbs**
PART C: **Finishing the Sentence**

PART A: Writing Sentences with Subjects and Verbs

Which of these groups of words is a sentence? Be prepared to explain your answers.

1. He left at 9:00 a.m.
2. The orange cheetah
3. Was swinging a gold cane
4. Scratches his head
5. My cousin teaches economics on Tuesdays.

○ In (2), you probably wanted to know what the "orange cheetah" did. The idea is not complete because there is no *verb*.

○ In (3), you probably wanted to know who "was swinging a gold cane." The idea is not complete because there is no *subject*.

○ In (4), you probably wanted to know who "scratches his head." The idea is not complete. What is missing?

○ But in sentences (1) and (5), you knew *who did what*. These ideas are complete. Why?

A *sentence* must have a *subject* and a *verb*.

Practice

All of these are pieces of sentences (*fragments*); they lack either a subject or a verb or both. Add either a subject or a verb or both in order to make the *fragments* into sentences.

21

1. stretched his neck to look out of the window

   rewrite: _____

2. the boy with the red hair

   rewrite: _____

3. one of the cockroaches

   rewrite: _____

4. was painting the bookcase green

   rewrite: _____

5. one by one

   rewrite: _____

6. feels as if he could eat a horse

   rewrite: _____

7. the yellow pad with lines

   rewrite: _____

8. his uncle, the one who works in the store,

   rewrite: _____

9. is hoping to go to college next fall

   rewrite: _____

10. seems to like to play baseball on Saturday

   rewrite: _____

11. faster and faster

   rewrite: _____

12. feels tired

   rewrite: _____

PART B: Writing Sentences with Complete Verbs

DON'T BE FOOLED . . .

> (1)   She leaving for the city.
> (2)   The students gone to the cafeteria for dessert.

- ○ *Leaving* seems to be the verb in (1).
- ○ *Gone* seems to be the verb in (2).

But . . .

- An *-ing* word is not by itself a verb.
- A past participle (*gone*) is not by itself a verb.

---

(1)   She $\left.\begin{array}{c} \textit{is} \\ \textit{was} \end{array}\right\}$ leaving for the city next week.

(2)   The students $\left.\begin{array}{c} \textit{have} \\ \textit{had} \end{array}\right\}$ gone to the cafeteria for dessert.

- An *-ing word,** in order to be a *verb,* must be combined with some form of *to be:*

  was hoping
  were watching
  are jogging
  is picking
  am going
  have been happening

- The past participle,† in order to be a *verb,* must be combined with some form of *to have* or *to be:*

  have grown
  is thrown
  has been
  had seen
  are taught
  has written
  was stolen
  were forgotten

Practice   1

All of these are pieces of sentences (*fragments*); they have only a partial or incomplete verb. Complete the verb in order to make these *fragments* into sentences.

1. The spotted cats creeping in the underbrush.

   rewrite: _____

2. They painting the flagpole a bright yellow.

   rewrite: _____

*For detailed explanation of these verb forms, see Chapter 10.

†For detailed explanation of these verb forms, see Chapter 8.

3. The children grown a lot this past year.

   rewrite: _____

4. By six, he already walking to his next class.

   rewrite: _____

5. I seen her here before.

   rewrite: _____

6. I going to be a doctor.

   rewrite: _____

7. She playing her guitar when the mouse made its appearance.

   rewrite: _____

8. He born in Toronto, Canada.

   rewrite: _____

9. We shown around his new house.

   rewrite: _____

10. By the time I arrived, he already gone.

    rewrite: _____

11. These photographs taken last year.

    rewrite: _____

12. On Thursday, they leaving for Europe.

    rewrite: _____

Practice 2

All of these are pieces of sentences (*fragments*); they lack a subject and they contain only a partial verb. Make these *fragments* into sentences by adding a subject and by completing the verb.

1. Walking down the street.

   rewrite: _____

2. Been there for two years.

   rewrite: _____

3. Finishing the term paper now.

   rewrite: _____

4. Gone over the fence for a home run.

   rewrite: _____

5. Written three novels in two months.

    rewrite: _____

6. Swimming all afternoon at Coney Island.

    rewrite: _____

7. Seen them at the movies twice so far.

    rewrite: _____

8. Shaking him hard in order to wake him up.

    rewrite: _____

9. Spoken to him about this matter before.

    rewrite: _____

10. Chosen a good location for the store.

    rewrite: _____

11. Doing a good job.

    rewrite: _____

12. Forgotten to bring the car keys.

    rewrite: _____

PART C: Finishing the Sentence

Can these ideas stand by themselves?

1. After they left the party . . .
2. When she came in . . .
3. Because he was happy . . .
4. Although I am tired . . .
5. While he studied the drawings . . .

Note that in all five examples you expect some idea to complete the thought. "When she came in" what happened? "Because he was happy" then what? The above thoughts have a subject and verb (find them), but they cannot stand alone as sentences because you expect some idea to complete the thought.*

Make all the above *fragments* into sentences by adding a complete thought to them.

Example: After they left the party, *we had a good time.*

1. _____

2. _____

*See Chapter 12 for more work on this kind of sentence.

3. _____

4. _____

5. _____

Can these ideas stand by themselves?

1. People who always lie . . .
2. A man that hopes for the best . . .
3. A teacher who does a good job . . .
4. Swimming, which is good exercise, . . .
5. Apples that have been left out too long . . .

You expect something to follow in all these sentences. *People who always lie are what?* Perhaps, *People who always lie make bad friends* or *People who always lie are my favorite kind.* In either case, the sentence has to be completed because the thought was left hanging.*

Complete these *fragments*.

Example: People who always lie *can't be trusted.*

1. _____

2. _____

3. _____

4. _____

5. _____

Practice

Rewrite all of these examples into complete sentences.

1. After we spoke on the telephone.

   rewrite: _____

2. Although he gets good marks. He doesn't know much about life.

   rewrite: _____

3. I do not love him anymore. Not as I used to.

   rewrite: _____

4. People running, screaming and crying.

   rewrite: _____

*See Chapter 15 for more work on this kind of sentence.

5. Felt terrible.

   rewrite: _____

6. Books that are too long.

   rewrite: _____

7. He is an active member. Of the Young Lords.

   rewrite: _____

8. If you say that once more.

   rewrite: _____

9. Over the river and through the woods.

   rewrite: _____

10. During the lecture, which lasted four hours.

    rewrite: _____

11. Patients in the wards sitting around all day with nothing to do.

    rewrite: _____

12. Friends who are always there when you need them.

    rewrite: _____

13. Trying to do his best.

    rewrite: _____

14. A man who is always on time.

    rewrite: _____

15. Because the music is soft and the lights are softer.

    rewrite: _____

16. Running all the way.

    rewrite: _____

17. Seems to know French.

    rewrite: _____

18. Faster and faster.

    rewrite: _____

19. If Robert goes to college this year.

    rewrite: _____

20. Killing me softly with his song.

    rewrite: _____

5

THE SMOOTH SENTENCE (Parallelism)

PART A: **Defining and Spotting Parallelism**
PART B: **Writing Parallels**
PART C: **Using Parallelism for Special Writing Effects**

PART A: Defining and Spotting Parallelism

Read each pair below carefully:

---

(1) I came. I would see and be conquering.
(2) *I came. I saw. I conquered.*

(3) Jeanne is both an artist and she spends time at athletics.
(4) Jeanne is both *an artist* and *an athlete*.

(5) He slowed down and came sliding and the winning run was scored.
(6) He *slowed* down, *slid,* and *scored* the winning run.

Do (2), (4), and (6) sound more smoothly and clearly written to you?

Sentences (2), (4), and (6) each repeat similar words or phrases to show similar ideas.

This technique is called _parallelism_.

The italicized parts of (2), (4), and (6) are _parallel_.

○ Can you see how *I came, I saw,* and *I conquered* in (2) are parallel? Each short sentence has the subject *I* and a verb in simple past tense.
○ In (4), how are *an artist* and *an athlete* parallel? How are the words alike?
○ In (6), how are *slowed, slid,* and *scored* parallel?

Two or more single words (*cries and whispers*) can be parallel as can entire sentences (*His face grew red. His voice grew loud.*).

But remember, parallel words must have the same grammatical form—a noun must be balanced with a noun, a past tense verb with a past tense verb.

Practice

Read through the parallel series below and circle the element in each that **is not parallel.**

Example: blue

    red

    colored like rust

    purple

1. camping
   boat rides
   hiking
   skiing

2. They raise corn and wheat.
   They make their own wine.
   They are digging for clams.

3. in the pit of his stomach
   across his forehead
   his eyes
   through his veins

4. painting pictures
   two boxes of watercolors
   a large sketch pad
   crayons

5. loneliness
   despair
   sadly

6. wrapped in furs
   adorned with jewels
   into the Rolls Royce
   bathed in perfume

7. power
   courage
   honesty
   strong

8. fly
   fluttered
   faded
   fell

9. rib restaurants
   chicken shacks
   eating meat pies
   soul food shops

10. carefree in the summer
    in the fall
    depressed in the winter
    renewed in the spring

PART B: Writing Parallels

Now, rewrite each of the following and use *parallelism* to accentuate the parallel ideas.

Example: We would break some windows, hopped a few trains. We had a few fights.

Rewrite: *We broke a few windows, hopped a few trains, and had a few fights.*

1. Tom enjoys swimming, and he likes to skate too.

   Rewrite: _Tom enjoy swimming and skateing_

2. He wore a green suede jacket, and his shirt was flowered. He was wearing platform shoes, multicolored.

   Rewrite: _He was wearing a green suede jacket, flowered shirt and an multicolored platform shoes_

3. At 16, I was full of wildness, outspoken, and I was an uncaring person.

   Rewrite: _at 16, I was wild, outspok and an uncaring pers_

4. The work was difficult and there was danger in it.

   Rewrite: _The work was difficult_

5. Like many women, she had several roles: wife, mother, going to school, job. _She like many women, Had several roles,_

   Rewrite: _a wife, mother, student and a job_

6. When the teacher left the room, I talked loudly, was fighting with my classmates and would throw paper airplanes and even climbed on the desks.

   Rewrite: _I talked loudy, fighting with my classma throw paper airplanes and even climbe_

7. When I disobeyed, my parents punished me: no going out, I couldn't talk on the telephone, and was not allowed to have company.

   Rewrite: _When I disobeyed my parents, they punish me by not allowed me to have company, going out and talk on the telephon_

8. Slowly, with ease, and soundless, the dancers moved offstage.

   Rewrite: _Slowly with ease, the dancer moved off soundless_

9. The drums pounded, did throb, were rising and falling.

   Rewrite: _The drum pounded throb, rise fall_

10. Good writing must be honest, have freshness, and precise words.

    Rewrite: _Good writing must be hones, freshnes precisely_

11. My son wants to be either a fireman or fly planes.

    Rewrite: _____

12. The students were more interested in dates with girls than in studying math.

    Rewrite: _____

Practice

Below are the *skeletons* of sentences; fill in the blanks in each sentence with **parallel words or phrases** of your own. Be creative. Take care that your sentences make sense and that your parallels are truly parallel.

Example: I feel *rested* and *happy*.

1. Subways are _____ , _____ ,

   and _____ .

2. At those parties, we had lots of fun. We _____dance_____ ,

   ____drink____ , and ____talk____ .

3. In high school ____The teacher teach____ ,

   but in college ____Thy teachy lectuva____ .

4. ____Needles____ and ____blood____

   make me nervous.

5. It is much harder to ____white____

   than to ____talk____ .

6. If you ____eat right____ and ____excisese____ ,
   you will feel healthy.

7. The way we dress reveals our ____personality____ , our

   _____ and our _____ .

8. Many city apartments are plagued by _____ ,

   _____ , and _____ .

9. When you _____ or _____ ,
   it is hard to find a good job.

10. It was a clear April day. In the park, ____children playing____ ,

    ____lovers kissing____ , and ____bird singing____ .

11. If you are a man in America, _____ ;

    if you are a woman in America, _____ .

12. Many college students _____ ,

    _____ , and _____ .

13. Bargain hunters either _____ or

    _____ .

14. O.J. Simpson is a man who _drink orange juice_ ,

    _____ , and who _kingston Henry_ .

15. When I write in class _____ ;

    when I write at home _____ .

PART C: Using Parallelism for Special Writing Effects

Here is one further use of parallelism.

> The handsome cowboy *saddled up, leaped onto his horse,* and _____ .

Now complete the sentence with each of the following parallel elements:

> and . . . *fell off.*
> *rode away from the land he loved.*
> *burped.*

- What effect does each ending have on you?
- Do you see how the order of parallel elements can affect your readers' responses?

By arranging the order of a parallel series, you can build dramatically toward the end:

> He *tensed* visibly, *slammed* his fist on the table, and *shouted*, "Shut up, you liars!"

Or, you can build up your readers' expectations and then use surprise for a humorous effect:

> He *tensed* visibly, *slammed* his fist on the table, and *forgot* what he wanted to say.

Practice

A. Write five sentences of your own, using parallelism to build toward a dramatic finish. *One sentence.*

1. _____

2. _____

3. _____

4. _____

5. _____

B. Write five sentences using parallelism to build toward a humorous or surprising finish. *One sentence.*

1. _____

2. _____

3. _____

4. _____

5. _____

UNIT II VERBS

6

PRESENT TENSE (Agreement)

PART A: Defining Agreement

A subject and a present tense verb agree if you use the *appropriate form* of the verb with your subject.

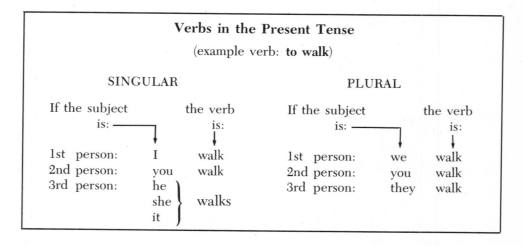

Verbs in the Present Tense
(example verb: **to walk**)

SINGULAR				PLURAL		
If the subject is: →		the verb is: ↓		If the subject is: →		the verb is: ↓
1st person:	I	walk		1st person:	we	walk
2nd person:	you	walk		2nd person:	you	walk
3rd person:	he she it	walks		3rd person:	they	walk

○ As you can see, the chart shows you what form of the verb to use for each kind of pronoun subject (we will discuss other kinds of subjects later).

34

Practice 1

Fill in the correct form of the verb in the blank space.

1. They **seem** tired.   He _____ tired .

2. We **hope** it is true.   She _____ it is true.

3. They **sing.**   He _____ .

4. She **decides** to go.   He _____ to go.

5. You **fall.**   He _____ .

6. I **laugh** often.   She _____ often.

7. We **fly.**   It _____ .

8. You **purchase** clothes.   He _____ clothes .

9. They **study** hard.   She _____ hard.

10. It **helps** me.   He _____ me.

The only time that you can add an *-s or -es* to a verb in the present tense is when the subject is a *third person singular (he, she, it).*

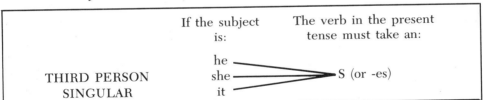

	If the subject is:	The verb in the present tense must take an:
THIRD PERSON SINGULAR	he she it	S (or -es)

Practice 2

Write in the correct form of the verb in the space at the right of the pronoun.

Example: **to see**
    I *see*
    they *see*
    she *sees*

to hope   **to live**   **to go**

he _____   I _____   he _____

they _____   she _____   you _____

it _____   he _____   we _____

to jump   **to hold**   **to read**

I _____   it _____   she _____

they _____   we _____   he _____

she _____   you _____   I _____

to write   **to do**   **to repair**

we _____   it _____   you _____

you _____   I _____   I _____

he _____   he _____   we _____

Practice 3

First underline the subject of each sentence below; then circle the correct verb form. Remember, if the subject of the sentence is a **he, she,** or **it** (third person singular), then there must be an -s or -es on the verb for it to **agree** with the subject.

1. They (look, looks) great.

2. In the afternoon, he (plays, play) basketball in the park.

3. I never (write, writes) my papers on time.

4. He always (write, writes) his papers on time.

5. She (plan, plans) to go to medical school in Mexico City.

6. He (gives, give) out the papers five minutes before the final begins.

7. I like that book because it (tells, tell) an exciting story.

8. If he (sleeps, sleep) too late, he (misses, miss) the show—it's as simple as that.

9. Although the soda looks good, it (taste, tastes) terrible.

10. I am taking the test later today, but I (think, thinks) I will do well.

11. We love exercise because it (help, helps) us lose weight.

12. She (reads, read) more than most people I (know, knows).

13. I am throwing out the old bookcase; it (messes, mess) up the modern look of my room.

14. She (jump, jumps) out of bed, (get, gets) dressed in a hurry, and (zooms, zoom) out of the house towards school, where she (puts, put) in a full day's work.

15. If you (want, wants), you can leave now.

16. They (seems, seem) tired.

17. Flowers grow in the spring; they (die, dies) in the winter.

18. Because my guitar is broken, it (sound, sounds) terrible.

19. I (drink, drinks) a quart of milk daily.

20. They (drink, drinks) a quart of milk daily.

21. He (drink, drinks) a quart of milk daily.

22. If she (wants, want) to get good grades, she has to get extra help.

23. We (light, lights) candles for dinner on Sunday.

24. You (knits, knit) beautiful sweaters.

25. She (smokes, smoke) too much, he also (smokes, smoke) too much, but I (hates, hate) smoking.

PART B: Troublesome Verb in the Present Tense: TO BE

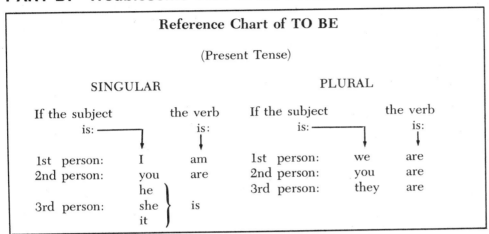

The chart may also be read like this:

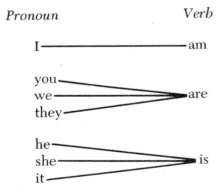

Practice   1

Fill in the correct form of **to be** in the space to the right of the subject. Use the chart—either one or both—to help you decide which form of the verb will agree with the subject.

1. he _____   4. I _____

2. we _____   5. she _____

3. you _____   6. we _____

7. it _____   14. she _____

8. he _____   15. it _____

9. you _____   16. she _____

10. we _____   17. he _____

11. they _____   18. we _____

12. we _____   19. they _____

13. you _____   20. you _____

Practice 2

Fill in the form of the verb **to be** that agrees with the subject. Use the charts.

1. They _____ ready to leave now if you _____ .

2. Because he _____ late, we _____ angry with him.

3. It _____ too cold to go for a walk, but she _____ a hardy soul and is going anyway.

4. We _____ sorry about your accident; you _____ certainly unlucky with cars.

5. Although I _____ sure about changing my career, it _____ still a big step for me to take.

6. She _____ from Puerto Rico and speaks perfect English; she _____ a truly amazing student.

7. We _____ in the same history class, but he _____ still rather unfriendly towards me.

8. They _____ good tutors.

9. She _____ a good tutor.

10. I _____ a good tutor.

11. Because you _____ an A student, we _____ proud to have you at the college.

12. It _____ unwise to drive on a slippery road if you _____ a generally nervous person.

13. I _____ so tired!

14. They _____ not willing to do all that extra work.

15. She _____ brighter than her older brother.

PART C: Troublesome Verb in the Present Tense: TO HAVE

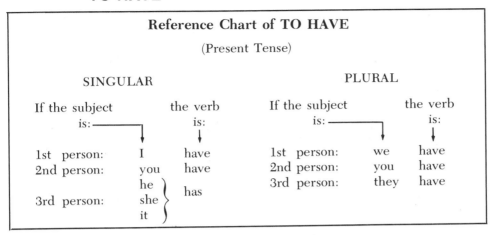

Reference Chart of TO HAVE

(Present Tense)

SINGULAR		PLURAL	
If the subject is:	the verb is:	If the subject is:	the verb is:
1st person: I	have	1st person: we	have
2nd person: you	have	2nd person: you	have
he		3rd person: they	have
3rd person: she }	has		
it			

The chart may also read like this:

Pronoun   *Verb*

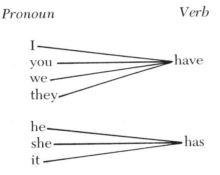

Practice   1

Fill in the correct form of **to have** in the space to the right of the subject. Use either chart to make sure the verb agrees with the subject.

1. he _____   9. we _____

2. we _____   10. you _____

3. you _____   11. they _____

4. I _____   12. we _____

5. they _____   13. they _____

6. she _____   14. you _____

7. it _____   15. she _____

8. they _____   16. he _____

17. we _____   19. we _____

18. they _____   20. it _____

Practice 2

Fill in the form of **to have** that agrees with the subject. Use the charts.

1. We _____ to leave early today.

2. You _____ three older brothers.

3. It _____ to be the right answer because I _____ no other.

4. They _____ little to do on Saturdays, but we _____ to do our homework for the week.

5. She _____ a good mind and, in addition, she _____ a strong sense of responsibility.

6. You _____ one and she _____ the other.

7. It _____ to be painted, and I _____ just the man to do it for you.

8. She _____ good instructors this semester.

9. They _____ no doubts, but he _____ some.

10. If I _____ the time, I will do that for you.

11. We _____ six books left to read for that course.

12. It _____ everything I have ever wanted in a house.

13. You _____ a good thing going for you.

14. He _____ a chance for the title in his next bout.

15. This booklet is good because it _____ looseleaf pages.

PART D: Troublesome Verb in the Present Tense: TO DO

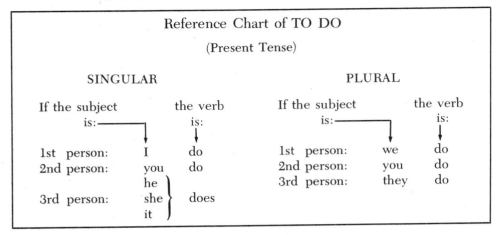

Reference Chart of TO DO

(Present Tense)

The chart may also be read like this:

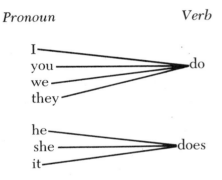

Practice 1

Fill in the correct form of **to do** in the space to the right of the subject. Use either chart and make sure the verb agrees with the subject.

1. he _____

2. we _____

3. she _____

4. I _____

5. you _____

6. they _____

7. he _____

8. we _____

9. she _____

10. they _____

11. I _____ enjoy

12. he _____ work

13. you _____ swim

14. they _____ conspire

15. she _____ move

16. we _____ laugh

17. they _____ win   19. I _____ succeed

18. it _____ shriek   20. he _____ have

As you see in 11 through 20 above, *do* and *does* are often used as helping verbs.

Practice 2

Fill in the correct form of **to do** (**do** or **does**) in the blank spaces in these sentences. Consult the chart if necessary.

1. He _____ his work on time.

2. If you _____ that, you will be sorry.

3. It _____ seem like a good day for a walk.

4. They _____ everything they can to conserve fuel.

5. I always _____ my best.

6. She _____ wildly colored oil paintings.

7. We most certainly _____ give private lessons.

8. He _____ spend a lot of time with his children.

9. You really _____ irritate me.

10. It _____ not work very well.

11. Every morning, we _____ exercises.

12. _____ she like tortillas? I _____ .

If you feel sure that you know how to use *do* and *does*, you are ready for *don't* and *doesn't*.

$$do + not = don't$$
$$does + not = doesn't$$

Practice 3

In the first column fill in the correct form of **to do** (**do** or **does**) to agree with the pronoun.

In the second column fill in the correct form of **to do** with the negative **not** (**don't** or **doesn't**).

Pronoun	Positive	Negative	Pronoun	Positive	Negative
1. he	*does*	*doesn't*	11. they	_____	_____
2. we	_____	_____	12. I	_____	_____
3. I	_____	_____	13. we	_____	_____
4. they	_____	_____	14. she	_____	_____
5. you	_____	_____	15. it	_____	_____
6. she	_____	_____	16. she	_____	_____
7. they	_____	_____	17. I	_____	_____
8. it	_____	_____	18. they	_____	_____
9. we	_____	_____	19. we	_____	_____
10. you	_____	_____	20. he	_____	_____

Practice 4

Fill in either **doesn't** or **don't** in each blank. Consult the chart if necessary.

1. It _____ work any longer.

2. If he _____ arrive soon, I'm leaving.

3. They _____ seem to care.

4. She _____ let anyone upset her.

5. I _____ want to leave this great party.

6. We _____ drive much now because of the fuel shortage.

7. Although you _____ like walking two miles a day to school, it certainly

    _____ do your health any harm.

8. He _____ usually go out much.

9. Because you _____ complete your homework, you _____ stand a good
   chance of passing the course.

10. They _____ have the time for baseball this Sunday.

11. It _____ use high-test gasoline.

12. She _____ play golf now that they _____ belong to the country club.

13. When he _____ try, he _____ succeed.

14. Although she _____ work here any longer, she drops in every week to say hello.

15. It _____ mean a thing if it _____ have a solid beat.

PART E: Transforming Subjects into Pronouns

So far, you have worked on pronouns as subjects (*I, you, he, she, it, we, they*) and how to make the verb agree with them.

Often, however, the subject of a sentence is not a pronoun (like those in the charts) but a different kind of word or words—like *dog, Sam, Sonia, Jose* and *Robert, swimming in cold weather*.

In order to be sure that your verb agrees with your subject, mentally transform the subject into a pronoun and then select the correct form of the verb.

TRANSFORMATION REFERENCE CHART	
If the subject is:	**it can be transformed into the pronoun:**
1. the speaker himself or herself	I
2. masculine and singular (**Bill, one man**)	he
3. feminine and singular (**Sondra, a woman**)	she
4. neither masculine nor feminine and singular (a thing or an action) (**this pen, love, running**)	it
5. a group which includes the speaker (I) (**the family and I**)	we
6. a group of persons or things not including the speaker (**tennis players, several pens**)	they
7. the person or persons spoken to	you

Practice

Transform these subjects into pronouns. Remember: if you add **I** to a group of persons, the correct pronoun for the whole group is **we**; if you add **you** to a group, the correct pronoun for the whole group is **you.**

Possible Subject	Transformed into	Pronoun
Example: Frank	=	_he_
1. a vase	=	_____
2. a vase and a chair	=	_____
3. Mr. Roberts	=	_____
4. her students	=	_____
5. Lydia	=	_____
6. a funny kitten	=	_____
7. his niece	=	_____
8. an old photograph	=	_____
9. Gene	=	_____
10. a large dog	=	_____
11. her radio	=	_____
12. her mother	=	_____
13. Sam and you	=	_____
14. mice	=	_____
15. a green Chevrolet	=	_____
16. the cat and dog	=	_____
17. Clara and I	=	_____
18. many friends	=	_____
19. a flowered hat	=	_____
20. the television set	=	_____
21. the pencils	=	_____
22. a palm tree	=	_____
23. Bill and I	=	_____
24. her slippers	=	_____

Possible Subject	Transformed into	Pronoun
25. Susan	=	_____
26. a textbook	=	_____
27. Jose and his family	=	_____
28. Susan and Richard	=	_____
29. an old uncle	=	_____
30. the clerks	=	_____
31. my father	=	_____
32. the library	=	_____
33. his cousins	=	_____
34. a dictionary	=	_____
35. Alan and I	=	_____

PART F: Practice in Agreement

Practice   1

Transform each subject into a pronoun. Then circle the present tense verb that agrees with that subject (use the reference chart if you need to).

Example: Harry = *he*   Harry (walk, (walks))
            Sam and I = *we*   Sam and I ((walk,) walks)

1. Jean = _____
2. The machine = _____
3. John and you = _____
4. John = _____
5. The dog and the cat = _____
6. The boys = _____
7. The boys and I = _____
8. Sylvia = _____

1. Jean (walk, walks).
2. The machine (is, are) noisy.
3. John and you (sings, sing) well.
4. John (seems, seem) sleepy.
5. The dog and the cat (plays, play).
6. The boys (thinks, think) it will work.
7. The boys and I (reads, read) a lot.
8. Sylvia (speaks, speak) softly.

9. This pen = _____

9. This pen (writes, write) well.

10. Hector, Sam and I = _____

10. Hector, Sam and I (likes, like) to play tennis.

11. My uncle = _____

11. My uncle (disappears, disappear) when there is work to do.

12. The typewriter and the ribbon = _____

12. The typewriter and the ribbon (is, are) worn out.

13. My father = _____

13. My father (walks, walk) too fast for me.

14. My jumpsuit = _____

14. My jumpsuit (has, have) to be cleaned.

15. The bread = _____

15. The bread (is, are) stale.

16. Sonia and Maria = _____

16. Sonia and Maria (goes, go) dancing every Saturday night.

17. My best friend and you = _____

17. My best friend and you (has, have) similar goals in life.

18. Swimming in shark-infested waters = _____

18. Swimming in shark-infested waters (is, are) dangerous.

19. Those plates = _____

19. Those plates (is, are) lovely.

20. His sister and I = _____

20. His sister and I often (travels, travel) together.

21. A good automobile = _____

21. A good automobile (lasts, last) a long time.

22. This short story = _____

22. This short story never (seems, seem) to end.

23. My niece = _____

23. My niece (am, is, are) two years old.

24. My nephews = _____

24. My nephews (is, are) in college.

25. Julio = _____

25. Julio (has, have) a good head for mathematics.

Practice 2

Circle the correct verb in each sentence below, making sure it agrees with its subject.

1. The children (loves, love) to paint with watercolors.
2. Miguel (reads, read) too fast.
3. He never (tries, try) to be something that he is not.
4. She and I (am, is, are) leaving now.
5. Sam and Bob (seems, seem) to be good friends.
6. The students (finds, find) that writing can be fun.
7. The fruit on the table (tastes, taste) good.
8. She (hopes, hope) to go to law school.
9. Latin music (appeal, appeals) to me.
10. The tutor in my English class always (participates, participate) in our discussions.
11. Our television set (has, have) to be repaired.
12. Helena (repairs, repair) televisions and radios like a professional.
13. Tests sometimes (gives, give) an indication of what a student has learned.
14. Dancing (relaxes, relax) me.
15. The good pianist always (practices, practice).

Practice 3

In each blank below, write the **present tense form of one of the verbs** from this list. Your sentences may be a little funny, just as long as each verb agrees with each subject.

to talk	to punch	to tickle	to drink
to kiss	to arrive	to sing	to dance

Many famous people _____ at the party. Joe Namath _____ the Mayor. Mick

Jagger and I _____ near the punchbowl, not far from Walt Frazier, who _____

with a small poodle. Several movie stars _____ in one corner of the room. Then, Tito

Puente _____ Ann Landers and everybody goes home.

Practice 4

The sentences which follow have singular subjects and verbs. To gain skill in verb agreement, rewrite each sentence, changing the subject **from the singular to the plural.** Then make sure the verb agrees with the new subject. Keep all verbs in the present tense.

Example: The boy runs.

Rewrite: The boys run.

1. My dog seems hungry.

   Rewrite: _____

2. The student is telling the truth.

   Rewrite: _____

3. The child learns to talk very rapidly.

   Rewrite: _____

4. During the second set, the drummer collapses on the stage.

   Rewrite: _____

5. The cow jumps over the moon.

   Rewrite: _____

6. The college offers many scholarships.

   Rewrite: _____

7. His room looks messy.

   Rewrite: _____

8. She runs the track in 6 minutes flat.

   Rewrite: _____

9. The infant makes funny gurgling noises.

   Rewrite: _____

10. My sofa is in bad shape.

    Rewrite: _____

Now rewrite each of the following sentences changing the subject **from the plural to the singular.** Then make sure the verb agrees with the new subject. Keep all verbs in the present tense.

1. My friends dance wildly at these parties.

   Rewrite: _____

2. They wonder what is wrong with her.

   Rewrite: _____

3. In the hospital, nurses carrying medicine walk the halls.

   Rewrite: _____

4. Those clouds indicate that a storm is coming.

   Rewrite: _____

5. My grandparents have a farm in Georgia.

   Rewrite: _____

6. The flowers smell sweet.

   Rewrite: _____

7. His friends are active politically.

   Rewrite: _____

8. The paintings add a look of charm to the room.

   Rewrite: _____

9. My pet guinea pigs eat raw eggs.

   Rewrite: _____

10. The offices are poorly lighted.

   Rewrite: _____

Practice 5

Rewrite this paragraph in the present tense. Do this by changing the verbs.

> Maria wanted to write plays for a living. People fascinated her. She studied them on the subway, at her job, and imagined what their lives were like, what their problems were. She told me that during spare moments at work, she made plays about them in her mind. Then every night for two hours, she wrote. I admired Maria, who always found time to do what she loved.

_____

_____

_____

_____

_____

_____

_____

_____

_____

PART G: Special Problems in Agreement

So far you have learned that if the subject of a sentence is third person singular *(he, she, it)* or a word that can be transformed into a *he, she,* or *it,* then the verb takes *-s or -es* in the present tense.

But there are some tricky cases in which you will need some additional knowledge and guidance before you can make your verb agree with your subject.

FOCUSING ON THE SUBJECT

> A box of Christmas lights is near the tree.

○ What *is* near the tree?
○ Don't be confused by the words that precede the verb—*of Christmas lights*.
○ Just one *box* is near the tree.
○ A *box* is the subject.
○ A *box* takes the third person singular—*is*.

A box [of Christmas lights] is near the tree.

subject   verb
(singular)   (singular)

> The children in the park play for hours.

○ Who *play for hours?*
○ Don't be confused by the words that precede the verb—*in the park.*
○ The *children* play for hours.
○ The *children* is the subject.
○ The *children* takes the third person plural—*play.*

The children [in the park] play for hours.

subject   verb
(plural)   (plural)

> The purpose of the themes is to give you practice writing.

○ What *is* to give you practice?
○ Don't be confused by the words that precede the verb—*of the themes.*
○ The *purpose* is to give you practice.
○ The *purpose* is the subject.
○ The *purpose* takes third person singular—is.

The purpose [of the themes] is to give you practice writing.

subject   verb
(singular)   (singular)

As you can see from the examples, sometimes what seems to be the subject is really not the subject. Groups of words beginning with *of, in, at, for, by, from, near*, etc. (called prepositional phrases) do not contain the subject of a sentence. The best way to find the subject of a sentence containing these phrases is to see *what makes sense as the subject* in terms of *what the sentence is saying.*

> My friends from the old neighborhood often $\begin{Bmatrix} \text{visits} \\ \text{visit} \end{Bmatrix}$ me.

- ○ Which makes sense?
- ○ What is the sentence saying?

| (1) My friends . . . visit me. | (2) The old neighborhood . . .visits me. |

- ○ Obviously, sentence (1) makes sense and expresses clearly the intention of the writer.

Practice   1

The words in these sentences are separated in such a way that you will be able to spot the subject quickly. Circle the subject, X-out the words that might confuse you (prepositional phrases) and choose the correct verb.

1. The purpose   of these tests   (is, are)   to help the instructor find out where you might need extra help.

2. The children   in the playground   (wants, want)   to leave at 7:00 p.m.

3. Plans   for the new campus   (is, are)   being made right now.

4. His year   in the public schools   (qualifies, qualify)   him for a permanent license.

5. The boys   from the local high school   (hopes, hope)   to organize a Spanish Culture Club.

Practice   2

Now try some similar examples. But here the sentences are not written with separations. It might help to cross out the words after **of, in, for,** etc. so you can spot the subject more easily.

1. The price of the repairs (seems, seem) out of line.
2. The wine in the bottles (tastes, taste) sour.
3. The strong smell of imported cheese (makes, make) my mouth water.
4. The cheese in the refrigerator (is, are) fresh.
5. The three adorable kittens on the rug (seems, seem) asleep.
6. The signs along the highway (blocks, block) everyone's view.
7. The toys on top of the dresser (belongs, belong) to my cousin.
8. The weight of the packing crates (is, are) hard to estimate.
9. The purpose of these meetings (is, are) to help the counselors do a better job.

10. The needs of this patient (requires, require) immediate attention.

11. The lamps in the stockroom (does, do) not work correctly.

12. The students in English 13 (wants, want) to give their instructor a present.

13. (Has, Have) the term papers of my last semester at college been filed in the Dean's Office?

14. The common cause for many illnesses (is, are) poor diet.

15. The function of his questions (remains, remain) unclear.

16. Those books on the shelf (looks, look) difficult.

17. The package for the student (is, are) here.

18. One of the maintenance men (promises, promise) to repair the stereo.

19. My relatives in Ireland (travels, travel) a great deal.

20. The machines by the door (appears, appear) old and useless.

SPOTTING SPECIAL SINGULAR SUBJECTS

```
┌──────────────────────────────────────────────────────────────┐
│   Either of the students    ⎫                                  │
│   Neither of the students   ⎪                                  │
│   Each of the students      ⎬  seems happy                     │
│   One of the students       ⎪                                  │
│   Every one of the students ⎭                                  │
└──────────────────────────────────────────────────────────────┘
```

o *Either, neither, each, one* and *every* are the real subjects of these sentences.

o *Either, neither, each, one* and *every* are special singular subjects and always take a singular verb.

o Note that what follows the *of*—the students—is not the subject.

Practice   1

Choose the correct verb in parentheses.

1. One of my friends (hopes, hope) to go to college this fall.

2. Neither of the books (is, are) right for the course.

3. Each of the choices (are, is) a good one.

4. Either of the students (does, do) excellent work.

5. Each of us (need, needs) a long vacation.

6. One of the cats (have, has) a cold.

7. Neither of them (looks, look) willing to do what he is supposed to.

8. One of these dresses (is, are) the right size.

9. Each of the desserts (does, do) have a lot of calories.

10. Neither of those pens (works, work) well.

11. Every one of my friends (goes, go) to college.

12. Neither of the contenders (is, are) really a good fighter.

13. One of the instructors (wants, want) to give A's to many students.

14. One of the doctors (does, do) not practice medicine any more.

15. Either of the fans (is, are) a nice gift.

Practice   2

Write eight sentences using the special singular subjects. Make sure your sentences are in the present tense.

1. _____

2. _____

3. _____

4. _____

5. _____

6. _____

7. _____

8. _____

USING THERE TO BEGIN A SENTENCE

> (1) *There* is a cat in the yard.
> (2) *There* are two cats in the yard.

○ Although sentences often begin with *there*, *there* cannot be the subject of a sentence.

○ Usually, the subject *follows* the verb in sentences that begin with *there*.

The way to find the real subject (so you will know how to make the verb agree) is to drop the *there* and rearrange the sentence.

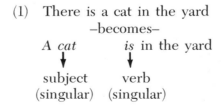

(1)   There is a cat in the yard
            –becomes–
   A cat   *is* in the yard
      ↓   ↓
   subject   verb
   (singular)   (singular)

(2)   There are two cats in the yard
            –becomes–
   Two cats   *are* in the yard
      ↓   ↓
   subject   verb
   (plural)   (plural)

Practice   1

Drop the **there,** rearrange the sentence, and choose the right form of the verb.

1. There (is, are) many things to do today.

2. There (is, are) only one thing to do today.

3. There (is, are) my best friend.

4. There (is, are) no way to climb this mountain by nightfall.

5. There (is, are) a great film on television this afternoon.

6. There (is, are) six students waiting for you.

7. There (is, are) dry clothes waiting for you in the bathroom.

8. There (is, are) a cactus and a geranium in the window.

9. There (is, are) a large chair in the corner.

10. There (is, are) many things to be learned from older people.

11. There (is, are) a goldfish and a guppy in the fishtank.

12. There (is, are) no reason for buying these expensive items.

13. There (is, are) two finals left to take.

14. There (is, are) children playing in the street. Be careful.

15. There (is, are) my slippers by the chair.

Practice   2

Write eight sentences beginning with **there.** Make sure your sentences are in the present tense.

1. _____

2. _____

3. _____

4. _____

5. _____

6. _____

7. _____

8. _____

USING WHO, WHICH, AND WHAT IN QUESTIONS

(1)   Who is the owner of this dog?

(2)   Who are the owners of this house?

(3)   What is the right answer?

(4)   Which are the right answers?

○ Sentences (1) and (3) have *singular verbs* because the subjects of these sentences are *owner* (1) and *answer* (3). If you get confused about what the subject is, turn the sentence around:

(1)   the owner of this dog is . . .

(3)   the right answer is . . .

○ Sentences (2) and (4) have a *plural verb* because the subjects of the sentences are *owners* (2) and *answers* (4). Turn the sentences around yourself to see how to get the correct verb.

(2)

(4)

Practice   1

Circle the correct verb.

1. What (has, have) they in their pockets?

2. Which (is, are) your slippers?

3. Who (is, are) the students in your class this semester?

4. What (seems, seem) to be the matter?

5. What (does, do) Juan say about that?

6. Who (wears, wear) that chartreuse poncho?

7. Which (is, are) the courses you want to take?

8. What (is, are) those books about?

9. Who (is, are) the women selling vegetables?

10. Who (appears, appear) to be the person best qualified for the job?

11. What (has, have) the parrot done to you?

12. Which (is, are) the famous painting?

Practice 2

Write three questions beginning with **who**, three beginning with **which**, and three beginning with **what**. Make sure your sentences are in the present tense.

1. _____

2. _____

3. _____

4. _____

5. _____

6. _____

7. _____

8. _____

9. _____

USING WHO, WHICH, AND THAT AS RELATIVES*

---

(1) I know a child who plays expert chess.

○ Sentence (1) uses the singular verb *plays* because *who* relates to *a child* (singular).

---

(2) Dogs that bite make me nervous.

○ Sentence (2) uses the plural verb *bite* because *that* relates to *dogs* (plural).

---

(3) Suede coats, which stain easily, should not be worn in the rain.

○ Sentence (3) uses the plural verb *stain* because *which* relates to

_____ (fill in)

*For work on writing relatives, see Chapter 15.

Practice

Write the word that the **who, which** or **that** relates (or refers) to in the sentences in the space at the right; then circle the correct form of the verb.

who, which, that
relates to . . .

Example: I like people *who* (is, (are)) clever.   *people*

1. Always take courses **that** (look, looks) difficult.   _____

2. I always avoid a person **who** (seems, seem) stuck-up.   _____

3. Judy has a grand piano **that** (costs, cost) $3,000.   _____

4. The apples **that** (is, are) too big for your mouth are   _____
   meant to be baked.

5. I can't find the books **that** (is, are) necessary.   _____

6. My uncles, **who** (loves, love) to read mystery stories,   _____
   are both detectives on the police force.

7. Don't chase a stray animal **that** (appears, appear)   _____
   frightened.

8. Swimming in polluted water, **which** (leads, lead) to   _____
   trouble, is a dumb thing to do.

9. People **who** (lives, live) in glass houses shouldn't   _____
   throw stones.

10. The walnuts **that** (has, have) green spots are poisonous.   _____

11. Dan likes women **who** (wear, wears) only   _____
    designer clothes.

12. Refined foods, **which** (include, includes) white   _____
    sugar and white flour, have few vitamins.

13. My brother likes music **that** (help, helps) him   _____
    relax.

14. I don't trust politicians **who** (promise, promises)   _____
    to solve all my problems.

15. Onions, **which** (survives, survive) the frost, may   _____
    be planted before the snow melts.

7
PAST TENSE

In the preceding lesson you learned how, in the present tense, to make verbs agree with their subjects.

This lesson will deal with verbs in the past tense. Verbs in the past tense express an action which occurred in the past.

PART A: Regular Verbs in the Past Tense

The italicized words in the following sentences are verbs in the past tense.

They *noticed* that the car was dented.

She *played* the guitar while we sang.

I *studied* yoga.

- What ending did all these verbs take? _____ (fill in)
- In general, then, how do you write most verbs in the past tense, by adding what kind of ending?
- Verbs which add *-d* or *-ed* to form the past tense are called *Regular Verbs*.

Practice 1

Some of the verbs in these sentences are in the past tense; others are in the present. Circle the verb. Write **present** in the column at the right if the verb is in the present tense. Write **past** if the verb is in the past tense (**-d** or **-ed** ending).

1. He walked down the street.   _____

2. She never walks down that street.   _____

3. Three children played in the park at the corner.   _____

4. I smiled at you yesterday.   _____

5. My father plays cards on the train.   _____

6. They hoped for the best.   _____

7. Her shoes look expensive.   _____

8. My suit looked cheap.   _____

9. That table shines beautifully.   _____

10. I shined my shoes.   _____

11. The student opened the book.   _____

12. My sons and daughter jumped rope in front of the house.   _____

13. The pencils dropped to the floor.   _____

14. His stereo sounds good.   _____

15. The visitors knock on the closed door.   _____

16. The plumber repaired the leaky pipe.   _____

17. These trees bloom every spring.   _____

18. She pinched his arm.   _____

19. The instructors marked the final.   _____

21. I sealed the envelopes.   _____

22. He sewed up the hole in his own shirt.   _____

23. These exercises last forever.   _____

Practice 2

In the left-hand column below are short sentences in the present tense. In the
column on the right, fill in the **past tense** form of each verb.

Present Tense   **Past Tense**

1. He decides.   1. He _____ .

2. Bob works hard.   2. Bob _____ hard .

3. They succeed.

4. He tries his best.

5. Maria answers the question.

6. I cry.

7. We relax at home.

8. It seems fine.

9. You act strangely.

10. I hope for the best.

11. She never laughs.

12. He always fakes it.

13. We play baseball.

14. The students study hard.

15. My friend jumps rope.

16. These people smile at me.

17. Her term paper looks good.

18. I repair the typewriter.

19. Her nephew loves her.

20. The instructor praises me.

21. I thank him.

22. The dogs bark at night.

23. His shoes pinch.

24. She nails the bookcase together.

25. They open the book.

3. They _____ .

4. He _____ his best.

5. Maria _____ the question.

6. I _____ .

7. We _____ at home.

8. It _____ fine.

9. You _____ strangely.

10. I _____ for the best.

11. She never _____ .

12. He always _____ it.

13. We _____ baseball.

14. The students _____ hard.

15. My friend _____ rope.

16. These people _____ at me.

17. Her term paper _____ good.

18. I _____ the typewriter.

19. Her nephew _____ her.

20. The instructor _____ me.

21. I _____ him.

22. The dogs _____ at night.

23. His shoes _____ .

24. She _____ the bookcase together.

25. They _____ the book.

As you can see from the exercise above, most verbs form the past tense by adding either -d or -ed.

As you can also see, in the past tense there is no problem of agreement (except for *to be*) as there was with verbs in the present tense. This is because verbs in the past tense have only one form no matter what the subject is.

Practice   3

A verb has been omitted from all of these sentences. Choose a verb from the column on the right. Then write the **past tense** form of this verb in the blank space.

1. As the flames _____ him, he _____ out of the window into the arms of the firemen below.

2. I _____ a ball at the dog; he _____ it and

   _____ it to me.

3. My father _____ the television set.

4. She _____ him on the cheek when she _____ the scholarship.

5. They _____ at the party until their feet _____ to move any longer.

6. I _____ to go to the University of Oregon.

7. Her father _____ the lobsters for an hour and a half.

8. On Thursday, he _____ football all day; on Sunday,

   he _____ a baseball game.

repair
broil
dance
umpire
kiss
want
approach
play
jump
refuse
receive
toss
return
accept

Practice   4

Put all these verbs in the past tense.

1. They _____ (play) at the Garden.

2. I _____ (work) until 3 A.M.

3. He _____ (litter) his own yard with junk.

4. The frogmen _____ (jump) into the pool.

5. When he _____ (turn) around, he saw me.

6. She _____ (empty) the closet in two seconds flat.

7. It _____ (happen) so fast, I could not react.

8. Raphael _____ (borrow) my turtle and my tape recorder.

9. She _____ (threaten) to drop him like a bad habit.

10. My friend and I _____ (discuss) politics all night.

11. When I was a child, I _____ (like) to climb trees.

12. His symptoms _____ (disappear) as soon as summer vacation began.

13. My cousin _____ (collect) hubcaps.

14. Sylvia _____ (admire) the graffiti on the D-train.

15. Tom and Marvin _____ (rob) a bank; later, they _____ (regret) it.

PART B: Irregular Verbs in the Past Tense

Read these sentences:

The children *grew* rapidly.

He *threw* the ball at the batter.

She *gave* him a dollar.

He *rode* from his farm into the town.

○ The italicized words in these sentences are also verbs in the past tense.

○ Do these verbs form the past tense by adding *-d* or *-ed*?

○ *Grew, threw, gave,* and *rode* are the past tense of verbs that do not add *-ed* or *-d* to form the past tense.

○ Verbs that do not add *-ed* or *-d* to form the past tense are called *Irregular Verbs*.

REFERENCE CHART: IRREGULAR VERBS

Simple Form	Past	Simple Form	Past
be	was, were	forget	forgot
become	became	forgive	forgave
begin	began	freeze	froze
blow	blew	get	got
break	broke	give	gave
bring	brought	go	went
build	built	grow	grew
buy	bought	have	had
catch	caught	hear	heard
choose	chose	hide	hid
come	came	hold	held
cut	cut	hurt	hurt
do	did	keep	kept
draw	drew	know	knew
drink	drank	lay	laid
drive	drove	lead	led
eat	ate	leave	left
fall	fell	let	let
feed	fed	lose	lost
feel	felt	lie	lay
fight	fought	make	made
find	found	meet	met
fly	flew	pay	paid

Simple Form	Past	Simple Form	Past
quit	quit	spend	spent
read	read	spring	sprang
ride	rode	stand	stood
rise	rose	steal	stole
run	ran	swim	swam
say	said	take	took
see	saw	teach	taught
seek	sought	tear	tore
sell	sold	tell	told
send	sent	think	thought
shake	shook	throw	threw
shine	shone	understand	understood
sing	sang	wake	woke (waked)
sit	sat	wear	wore
sleep	slept	win	won
speak	spoke	write	wrote

○ Can you divide these verbs according to the way they form the past tense?

○ For instance, *grow* and *blow* form the past tense by becoming *grew* and *blew*, or *come* and *drink* become *came* and *drank*.

○ You will find that some verbs don't fit into a particular category, that they have to stand alone, in no particular group.

Practice 1

Try your hand at grouping irregular verbs according to their spelling changes. First list in one group three or more verbs that change in similar ways. Then write out a generalization about the verbs in that group; that is, say how they are alike.

Start by adding more verbs to our example, Group I.

Example:

Group I   *grow   grew*   Generalization: Group I Verbs
            blow   blew
                                    Change **ow** *in simple form to* **ew** *in past*

_____

_____

Group II   Generalization: Group II verbs

_____

_____

_____

_____

Group III   Generalization: Group III verbs

_____

_____

_____

_____

Group IV   Generalization: Group IV verbs

_____

_____

_____

_____

Group V   Generalization: Group V verbs

_____

_____

_____

_____

As you can see from your groups of verbs, it is easier to learn a few similarly changing verbs at once than to memorize each verb separately.

Practice 2

Fill in the correct form of the verb in the past tense. Don't guess; use the charts.

1. Yesterday the heavy fog _____ before noon. (rise)

2. We _____ in after you did. (come)

3. She _____ us a map of the shortest route. (draw)

4. She _____ two inches last year. (grow)

5. I _____ a letter to Joe yesterday. (send)

6. Who _____ the paper on the floor? (throw)

7. Who _____ the milk? (drink)

8. He _____ as fast as he could (run)

9. Radishes _____ up where we thought we had planted carrots. (spring)

10. I _____ him just ten minutes ago. (see)

11. Everyone _____ across the lake. (swim)

12. The accident happened just as we _____ along. (come)

13. You _____ a lie. (tell)

14. She _____ about it for a long time. (think)

15. It was so cold, I nearly _____ my toes. (freeze)

16. They always _____ the correct answers. (know)

17. She _____ the bat tightly. (hold)

18. The students _____ themselves out studying. (wear)

19. That gang _____ a lamppost. (steal)

20. When he saw the test, he _____ all the answers. (forget)

21. A student _____ to me yesterday. (speak)

22. At the party, the band _____ playing all night. (keep)

23. The doctor _____ sick all day. (feel)

24. My friend _____ a new coat last week. (buy)

25. At the dude ranch, we _____ for hours. (ride)

26. She _____ a short rest. (take)

27. You _____ your new coat. (tear)

28. Last summer, he _____ every day. (swim)

29. The dog walked in and _____ near the table. (sit)

30. These exercises really _____ me crazy. (drive)

Practice 3

Pick out the ten irregular verbs that give you the most trouble and list them here:

Simple	Past	Simple	Past
_____	_____	_____	_____
_____	_____	_____	_____
_____	_____	_____	_____
_____	_____	_____	_____
_____	_____	_____	_____

Now, write one paragraph in the past tense using *all ten* verbs!

PART C: Troublesome Verb in the Past Tense: TO BE

SINGULAR	PLURAL
1st person: I was _____	we were
2nd person: you were _____	you were
3rd person: he ⎫ she ⎬ was _____ it ⎭	they were

Note that the 1st and 3rd person singular forms are the same—*was.*

Practice   1

Fill in the correct form of the verb **to be** in the past tense—either **was** or **were:**

1. I _____ here two years ago.

2. They _____ very rude.

3. He _____ always on time.

4. Maria _____ his girlfriend in second grade.

5. The man and the woman _____ in Central Park.

6. You _____ right and I _____ wrong.

7. The record _____ beautiful.

8. The dog _____ happy.

9. I _____ glad to help you with your homework, but they _____ unwilling to try to do theirs.

10. You _____ a sight for sore eyes.

11. _____ they here or _____ she there?

12. Where _____ you?

13. Our friends _____ there, but where _____ Bob?

14. The weather _____ snowy and chilly today.

15. The sofa and the chair _____ the oldest pieces of furniture I owned.

16. Billie Jean King _____ number one for quite a while.

17. My cat _____ in the corner a minute ago.

18. My parents _____ on vacation last week in Taxco.

19. How _____ the movie last night?

20. My father _____ a track star when he _____ younger.

TO BE + NOT

Be careful of verb agreement if you use the past tense of *to be* with *not* as a contraction.

$$\text{was} + \text{not} = \text{wasn't}$$
$$\text{were} + \text{not} = \text{weren't}$$

Practice 2

Fill in either **wasn't** or **weren't**:

1. We went ice skating, but she _____ there.

2. Why _____ you here when I called?

3. They _____ happy with their grades.

4. He and I _____ in class yesterday.

5. You _____ where you were supposed to be.

6. The students _____ willing to pay tuition.

7. Jose and Maria _____ on speaking terms.

8. Television _____ around until the 1940's.

9. The dog _____ a pure bred.

10. My plants _____ expensive.

11. We _____ able to get tickets for the concert.

12. My pet snake _____ where I had left him.

13. The pizza _____ hot when we got it home.

14. These books _____ interesting.

15. Roberto _____ there early enough to get a haircut.

16. She _____ to be found anywhere.

17. Her brother _____ at the movie theatre.

18. She and I _____ happy as man and wife.

19. The show _____ very good.

20. Why _____ you there when I needed you?

PART D: Review

Practice 1

Fill in the past tense form of each verb. Some are regular, others irregular.

1. As a girl she _____ beautiful. (be)

2. The rabbit was run over as it _____ onto the highway. (dash)

3. Last week he _____ me permission. (give)

4. Someone _____ my telephone. (tap)

5. She _____ her money away on trifles. (throw)

6. When the solution was stirred, the lighter liquid _____ to the surface. (rise)

7. The thief _____ my pocketbook. (grab)

8. Then I _____ him down with a karate chop. (knock)

9. When we _____ home, we found the doors locked. (come)

10. Steve _____ much later. (apologize)

11. The lion _____ from a rocky ledge. (spring)

12. They _____ members of a motorcycle gang. (be)

13. The rockets _____ gloriously before losing power. (soar)

14. Gus _____ distracted and unhappy. (seem)

15. I thought you _____ doing that when you were five. (stop)

16. He _____ the potion and turned into a frog. (drink)

17. Mom always asked me, "Who _____ you that?" (teach)

18. The crowd of students _____ it happen. (see)

19. To preserve the fruit, we _____ it. (freeze)

20. The child _____ to move from his spot in the tree-house. (refuse)

21. They _____ him. (impeach)

22. When I _____ for assistance, he refused me. (ask)

23. The Rolling Stones _____ stones around the stage. (roll)

24. On that diet, she _____ two pounds in two years. (lose)

25. I got so sick of verbs that I _____ to take a break. (decide)

26. Say, hey, I _____ all A's. (get)

27. I _____ here on time; where _____ you? (be)

28. The bubbles _____ out of the window and we all _____ in amazement. (fly, gaze)

29. She _____ up all at once and _____ soon able to take care of herself. (grow, be)

30. He _____ angry because I _____ a new suit and _____ not consult him. (seem, buy, do)

31. They _____ too much and _____ home in a daydream state. (drink, drive)

32. If you _____ late, you will probably finish late. (begin)

33. The angry child _____ the toy and _____ sorry afterward; but his parents _____ him a new one and everyone _____ again. (break, be, buy, smile)

34. I _____ him when he _____ down to the grocery store and _____ his old friend Paul there. (see, run, meet)

35. Sam _____ the telephone box until he _____ his dime back, and then he

_____ the operator that the phone _____ out of order. (shake, get, tell, be)

Practice 2

Rewrite the paragraph below in the **past tense** by changing the verbs.

My class is a crazy group. Every day, one of us writes something and brings it to class. The other students interpret the poem or composition in any way they want to. They sing, dance, or act it out. Tony says that he has no talent, so he contributes by eating oranges in the back row. Nobody ever misses class; in fact, visitors often wander in and stay.

_____

_____

_____

_____

_____

_____

_____

_____

_____

_____

8

THE PAST PARTICIPLE IN ACTION

PART A: Defining the Past Participle

(1)   I have played baseball for years.

(2)   She has played baseball for years.

(3)   They have played baseball for years.

○ Each sentence above contains a two-part verb. Circle the *first* part or helping verb in each and write it here:

(1) _____ (fill in)

(2) _____ (fill in)

(3) _____ (fill in)

○ Underline the *second* part, or main verb, in each sentence. This word, a form of the verb *to play*, is the same in all three. Write it here:

_____ (fill in)

○ *Played* is called the past participle of *to play*.

Every verb has one form that can be combined with helping verbs like *has* and *have* to make verbs of more than one word.

This form is called the *past participle.*

The past participle never changes no matter what the subject, no matter what the helping verb.

PART B: Past Participles of Regular Verbs

Fill in the past participle in each series below:

Present Tense	Past Tense	Helper + Past Participle
(1) Beth dances.	(1) Beth danced.	(1) Beth has _____
(2) They decide.	(2) They decided.	(2) They have _____
(3) He jumps.	(3) He jumped.	(3) He has _____

○ Are the verbs *to dance, to decide,* and *to jump* regular or irregular? How do you know?

○ What ending does each verb take in the past tense? _____ (fill in)

○ Remember that any verb that forms its past tense by adding *-d* or *-ed* is called *regular.* What past participle ending does each verb take?

_____ (fill in)

○ The past tense and the past participle forms of each regular verb are the same!

Practice   1

The first sentence in each pair below contains a one-word verb in the past tense. Fill in the past participle of the same verb in the second sentence.

Example: Tom punched the man.

Tom has *punched* the man.

1. She designed jewelry all her life.

She has _____ jewelry all her life.

2. Tom always studied in the bathtub.

   Tom has always _____ in the bathtub.

3. The children snapped their gum.

   The children have _____ their gum.

4. I locked all the doors.

   I have _____ all the doors.

5. Sylvia tackled the man who took her purse.

   Sylvia has _____ the man who took her purse.

6. The television flickered for months.

   The television has _____ for months.

7. They campaigned for a victory.

   They have _____ for a victory.

8. Mrs. Jones wrapped her baby in a yellow shawl.

   Mrs. Jones has _____ her baby in a yellow shawl.

9. The kitten scampered out the door.

   The kitten has _____ out the door.

10. The eggshell cracked.

    The eggshell has _____ .

The past participle of a regular verb ends in -ed, just like its past tense form.

Practice 2

Write the missing two-part verb in each sentence below; use the helping verb **has** or **have** and the past participle of the verb in parentheses.

Example: He *has walked* (to walk) a mile today.

1. André ___ _____ (to answer) the question.

2. They ___ _____ (to perform) in several musicals this year.

3. The interested students ___ already _____ (to turn) in their projects.

4. This mixture ___ _____ (to reach) the boiling point.

5. The swimmers ___ all _____ (to shave) their heads.

6. Professor Simmons ___ _____ (to lecture) until she is hoarse.

7. This bouquet of roses ___ _____ (to wither) quickly.

8. The paper factories ____ _____ (to disturb) the ecological balance.

9. Few women astronauts ____ _____ (to apply) for the job.

10. So, you ____ finally _____ (to change) your mind.

11. Until this event, the political climate ____ _____ (to seem) calm.

12. This ____ _____ (to happen) before.

13. The police ____ _____ (to finish) their investigation.

14. The children ____ _____ (to name) every puppy in the litter.

15. So far, only three students ____ _____ (to qualify) for the position.

PART C: Past Participles of Irregular Verbs

Present Tense	Past Tense	Helper + Past Participle
(1) He sees.	(1) He saw.	(1) He has seen.
(2) I take vitamins.	(2) I took vitamins.	(2) I have taken vitamins.
(3) We sing.	(3) We sang.	(3) We have sung.

- ○ Are the verbs *to see*, *to take*, and *to sing* regular or irregular?
- ○ Like all irregular verbs, *to see*, *to take*, and *to sing* do not add -ed to show past tense.
- ○ Most irregular verbs in the past are also irregular in the past participle—like *seen*, *taken*, and *sung*.

Grouping Irregular Verbs

Irregular verbs change their spelling in irregular ways, so there are no rules to explain their changes. However, there *are* patterns and groups of irregular verbs that can help you learn the changes.

REFERENCE CHART: IRREGULAR VERBS

Simple Form	Past	Past Participle
be	was, were	been
become	became	become
begin	began	begun
blow	blew	blown
break	broke	broken
bring	brought	brought
build	built	built

Simple form	Past	Past Participle
buy	bought	bought
catch	caught	caught
choose	chose	chosen
come	came	come
cut	cut	cut
do	did	done
draw	drew	drawn
drink	drank	drunk
drive	drove	driven
eat	ate	eaten
fall	fell	fallen
feed	fed	fed
feel	felt	felt
fight	fought	fought
find	found	found
fly	flew	flown
forget	forgot	forgotten
forgive	forgave	forgiven
freeze	froze	frozen
get	got	gotten
give	gave	given
go	went	gone
grow	grew	grown
have	had	had
hear	heard	heard
hide	hid	hidden
hold	held	held
hurt	hurt	hurt
keep	kept	kept
know	knew	known
lay	laid	laid
lead	led	led
leave	left	left
let	let	let
lie	lay	lain
lose	lost	lost
make	made	made
meet	met	met
pay	paid	paid
quit	quit	quit
read	read	read
ride	rode	ridden
rise	rose	risen
run	ran	run
say	said	said
see	saw	seen
seek	sought	sought
sell	sold	sold
send	sent	sent
shake	shook	shaken
shine	shone	shone
sing	sang	sung
sit	sat	sat
sleep	slept	slept
speak	spoke	spoken
spend	spent	spent
spring	sprang	sprung

Simple Form	Past	Past Participle
stand	stood	stood
steal	stole	stolen
swim	swam	swum
take	took	taken
teach	taught	taught
tear	tore	torn
tell	told	told
think	thought	thought
throw	threw	thrown
understand	understood	understood
wake	woke (waked)	woken (waked)
wear	wore	worn
win	won	won
write	wrote	written

○ Can you divide these verbs according to the way they form the past and past participle?

○ For example, does the spelling of *ring* change to show the past? To show the past participle?

○ How does the spelling of *sing* change to show the past and then the past participle?

○ Since *ring* and *sing* change their spelling in similar ways, they may be placed into the same *verb group*. Verbs in the *ring-sing* group change the middle vowel from *i* in simple to *a* in past to *u* in the past participle.

○ What other verbs from the chart might belong to this group?

Practice   1

To help you learn the irregular verbs, try your hand at grouping them according to their spelling changes. First, list in one group two or more verbs that are alike. Then write out a generalization about the verbs in that group; that is, say how they are alike, what they have in common.

Start by adding three or so more verbs to our example, Group I. Then see how many more verb groups you can find.

Example:

Group I:	*ring*	*rang*	*rung*	Generalization: Group I verbs
	sing	*sang*	*sung*	Change "i" in the simple form to "a" in the past, to "u" in the past participle
	begin	*began*	*begun*	

Group II: Generalization: Group II verbs

_____

_____

_____

_____

Group III: Generalization: Group III verbs

_____

_____

_____

_____

Group IV: Generalization: Group IV verbs

_____

_____

_____

Group V: Generalization: Group V verbs

_____

_____

_____

_____

Of course, you can't list all the verbs in all the groups. But what you have is a good start. Obviously, it is easier to study the verbs in groups than to attempt to learn the changes one by one.

Practice   2

The first sentence in each pair contains an irregular verb in the past tense. Fill in **has** or **have** plus the past participle of the same verb to complete the second sentence.

Example: I ate too much.
            I *have eaten* too much.

1. He chose to go with us.

    He ____ _____ to go with us.

2. They found math difficult.

    They ____ _____ math difficult.

3. She did her best.

   She ___ _____ her best.

4. John ran out the door.

   John ___ _____ out the door.

5. The woman fell on the icy sidewalk.

   The woman ___ _____ ___ on the icy sidewalk.

6. All of us slept very soundly in the country.

   All of us ___ _____ very soundly in the country.

7. Jose drove everyone home.

   Jose ___ _____ everyone home.

8. The survivors lost their sense of direction.

   The survivors ___ _____ their sense of direction.

9. I went shopping.

   I ___ _____ shopping.

10. Your writing began to improve.

    Your writing ___ _____ to improve.

Now you will be given only the first sentence with its one-word verb in the past tense. Rewrite the entire sentence, changing the verb to a two-word verb: **has** or **have** plus the past participle of the main verb.

Example: He took the giraffes with him.
   He has taken the giraffes with him.

1. I forgot to buy milk.

   _____

2. Leslie hid her money in the refrigerator.

   _____

3. The lecture was tedious.

   _____

4. At last, the police caught the thief.

   _____

5. Jane became more self-assured.

   _____

6. Anais tore pages from her diary.

   _____

7. They built a new city on the ruins of the old one.

   _____

8. They drank too much wine.

_____

9. We flew to California for the weekend.

_____

10. The heavy fog over the city rose.

_____

Practice 3

For each verb below, fill in the present tense (3rd person singular form), the past tense, and the past participle.

Simple	Present Tense (he, she, it)	Past Tense	Past Participle
know	*knows*	*knew*	*known*
break			
answer			
do			
swim			
bring			
flow			
fall			
feel			
take			
manage			
freeze			
give			
sell			
make			
force			
hold			
go			

Simple	Present Tense (he, she, it)	Past Tense	Past Participle
think			
say			
buy			
blow			
see			

Practice 4

Complete each sentence by filling in the helping verb **to have** and the past participle of the verb in parentheses.

Examples: Sheila *has done* (to do) her job well.
We *have watched* (to watch) the game.

1. Larry and Marsha _____ (to break) their engagement.

2. _____ you _____ (to finish) that book yet?

3. _____ you _____ (to take) the cat for its piano lesson?

4. The union _____ (to decide) to strike.

5. Lucy _____ (to scare) us like this before.

6. _____ they ever _____ (to go) to camp for the summer?

7. Jim _____ (to buy) every violin concerto in the store.

8. The woman _____ (to feed) the goldfish too much; now they must diet.

9. This cool weather _____ (to surprise) everyone.

10. The photographer _____ (to shoot) a series of pictures.

11. That man _____ (to run) around the block ten times!

12. Our class _____ (to write) some fine essays and stories.

13. They _____ (to think) deeply about their philosophies of life.

14. _____ you _____ (to check) the engine?

15. The management of this theater _____ never _____ (to allow) smoking.

16. Bill _____ (to cut) his hand.

17. Our state _____ (to legalize) abortion.

18. ____ Leslie _____ (to spell) every word correctly?

19. The students _____ (to accomplish) a great deal this term.

20. _____ you _____ (to master) the past participle forms?

Now check your work in the preceding exercises, or have it checked. Do you see any patterns in your errors? Do you tend to miss regular or irregular verbs? Refer to your grouping of irregular verbs; do you tend to miss verbs in the same group?

   To help you learn, copy all four forms of each verb that you missed into the review chart below and use it for study.

PERSONAL REVIEW CHART

Simple	Present Tense (he, she, it)	Past Tense	Past Participle

PART D: Using the Present Perfect Tense (have or has + past participle)

So far you have practiced writing verbs in the Present Perfect Tense: present tense of *to have* + *past participle.*

Present Perfect Tense

I **have** spoken	we **have** spoken
you **have** spoken	you **have** spoken
he she } **has** spoken it	they **have** spoken

Now let us look at the way this tense should be used:

---

(1) They *sang* together last Saturday.

---

(2) They *have sung* together for three years now.

○ The past tense verb *sang* in (1) above tells us that they sang together on one occasion in the past; the action began and ended in the past, last Saturday.

○ To say they *have sung* together tells us something entirely different: that they first sang together in the past and they *have continued to sing together until now.*

○ *Have sung* is Present Perfect Tense.

---

(3) My dog *ate* a box of soap flakes.

---

(4) My dog *has eaten* a box of soap flakes.

○ Which dog is probably still sick?

○ In (3), the dog's action began and ended at some time in the past. Perhaps it was ten years ago that the dog *ate* soap flakes.

○ The verb *has eaten* in (4) implies that while the action occurred in the past, it *has just happened,* and something had better be done *now* for the poor dog.

○ *Has eaten* is Present Perfect Tense.

Use the Present Perfect Tense to show that an action began in the past and has continued until now ("They have sung together for three years.") or that an action has just happened ("My dog has eaten soap flakes.").

Practice

Paying close attention to meaning, decide whether past tense or present perfect tense best completes each sentence and expresses its meaning.

Example: Ten years ago, American automobiles ((were), have been) very different from those of today.

1. When I was a child in Puerto Rico, Angel and I (walked, have walked) to school every day.

2. At that time, we usually (went, have gone) barefoot.

3. Blue sea still rolls on white sand as it (did, has done) for centuries.

4. When Tim was twenty years old, he (moved, has moved) to New York City.

5. Tim is my next door neighbor; he (lived, has lived) here for five years.

6. Couples strolled along the boardwalk, and children (rode, have ridden) their bicycles.

7. Police silently entered the bar and (hurried, have hurried) through the curtains into the back room.

8. Georgina works at the hospital; she (worked, has worked) there for five years.

9. On Thursday our group (visited, has visited) the planetarium.

10. Joe made a scene and (said, has said) he wouldn't cook dinner.

PART E: Using the Past Perfect Tense (had + past participle)

Use the present tense of *to have* in writing the Present Perfect Tense and the past tense of *to have* in writing Past Perfect Tense.

Past Perfect Tense	
I **had** spoken	we **had** spoken
you **had** spoken	you **had** spoken
he she } **had** spoken it	they **had** spoken

Let us see how this tense is used and how it *differs* from Present Perfect.

(1) Because Linda *has broken* her leg, she *wears* a cast.

(2) Because Bob *had broken* his leg, he *wore* a cast for six months.

○ Linda now *wears* (present tense) a cast on the leg that she *has broken* (present perfect tense) at some time *before now.*

○ Sentence (2), however, occurred entirely in the past. At some time in the past Bob *wore* (past tense) a cast on the leg that he *had broken* (past perfect tense) at some time *before that.*

When you are writing in the past tense, use Past Perfect Tense to show that something happened at an even earlier time.

As a general rule, Present Perfect Tense is used in relation to present tense, and Past Perfect Tense is used in relation to past tense. Read these pairs and note the time relations:

---

(1) Sid *says* (present) he *has found* (present perfect) a good job.
(2) Sid *said* (past) he *had found* (past perfect) a good job.

---

(3) Grace *tells* (present) us she *has won* (present perfect) the lottery.
(4) Grace *told* (past) us she *had won* (past perfect) the lottery.

Practice 1

Match present tense with Present Perfect Tense and past tense with Past Perfect Tense below. Write in either the Present Perfect or the Past Perfect Tense of the verb in parentheses to complete each sentence.

1. The jurors leave each night, knowing they ____ _____ (to do) their best.

2. The jurors left each night, knowing they ____ _____ (to do) their best.

3. The baby ____ _____ (to fall) down; I hope she is not hurt.

4. The baby ____ _____ (to fall) down; I hoped she was not hurt.

5. As Leroi entered the beautiful room, he knew he ____ _____ (to be) there before.

6. As Leroi enters the beautiful room, he knows he ____ _____ (to be) there before.

7. He throws a knife at my feet and says he ____ _____ (to come) to settle an old debt.

8. He threw a knife at my feet and said he ____ _____ (to come) to settle an old debt.

9. Ted ____ _____ (to forget) to pay his electric bill; he was unable to watch the news.

10. Ted ____ _____ (to forget) to pay his electric bill; he is unable to watch the news.

Practice 2

Read these carefully for time and meaning. Fill in the Present Perfect or Past Perfect Tense of the verb in parentheses, whichever best expresses the time and meaning.

1. My cat ____ _____ (to drink) bubble bath; I am very worried about her.

2. I look forward to my trip this summer, since I _____ never _____ (to be) out of the city before.

3. Sonia went to Puerto Rico for Christmas last year. She ____ _____ (to go) to Mexico the year before that.

4. Kenneth Brown plans to retire next year from the college where he _____

   _____ (to teach) chemistry for 25 years.

5. This will be my very first camera; I ____ never _____ (to own) a camera before.

6. The old man ate his meal as though he ____ never _____ (to eat) before.

7. If Doris ____ already _____ (to make) the dessert, please let me know right away.

8. ____ you ever _____ (to wonder) why Marlene always wears radishes in her ears? I have.

9. If Shakespeare ____ _____ (to live) to see the twentieth century, what do you think he would say?

10. If only I ____ _____ (to know) that the exam was today, I would have studied.

11. Ten years ago, on my 16th birthday, I bought myself a car; I _____

    _____ (to want) a car for about 15 years before that.

12. Congratulations! You ____ _____ (to complete) a very difficult exercise.

PART F: To Be + Past Participle: Acts Upon the Subject

> (1) We were robbed by a street gang.

- ○ *We* is the subject of sentence (1), and the verb has two parts: helping verb *were* and the past participle *robbed*.
- ○ Who or what were *robbed*? Who committed the crime?
- ○ Note that *we*, the subject, does not act but is *acted upon* by the verb. *By a street gang* tells us who committed the crime.

We *were robbed* by a street gang.

> (2) Every year Joe is chosen to speak.

---
(3) Every year Carol has chosen the band.

- Who *is acted upon*, Joe or Carol?
- Joe, the subject of (2), *is chosen*, is acted upon, although we do not know by whom.
- Carol, on the other hand, *has chosen* (present perfect tense) something; she has acted.
- When the helping verb is a form of *to be* instead of *to have*, the subject of the sentence is acted upon.

When *to be* is combined with the *past participle*, the subject of the sentence does not act, but is acted upon by the verb.

When the subject is acted upon, it is *passive* and the verb (to be + past participle) has *passive voice*.

Using the *passive voice* emphasizes the receiver of the action rather than the doer.

Practice

In each sentence below, put a box around the subject and underline both parts of the passive verb. Then draw an arrow from the verb to the word it acts upon.

Example: A dance *was held* every month by our club.

1. Our argument was soon forgotten.

2. Visitors to the museum are permitted to bring cameras.

3. Many old customs are destroyed by technology.

4. My fall on the ice was loudly cheered by my friends.

5. Jennifer was last seen riding her pet camel.

6. These letters were written many years ago.

7. If help is offered, accept it.

8. My subscription was cancelled by the billing department.

9. These curtains were torn by the cat.

10. The children are not allowed to stay up past eight.

11. As a child, Bob was pushed from one home to another.

12. I was thrilled by the instructions on the final.

PART G: Linking Verb + Past Participle: Describes the Subject

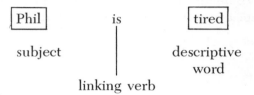

(1) Phil is tired.	(2) I felt amazed.

- ○ In these sentences, the subjects neither act nor are acted upon. There is really no action.
- ○ *Tired* and *amazed* are past participles, but they describe rather than act.
- ○ In (1), *tired* describes the subject *Phil. Is* works like a linking verb to connect them.
- ○ In (2), *amazed* describes the subject *I.* Linking verb *felt* connects them.

Phil   is   tired

subject   descriptive word

linking verb

Words like *tired* and *amazed* are really past participles of regular verbs (to tire, to amaze) that are often used as descriptive words.

To be most often links such descriptive past participles with the subjects they describe, but there are a few other linking verbs that can link subjects and descriptive past participles.

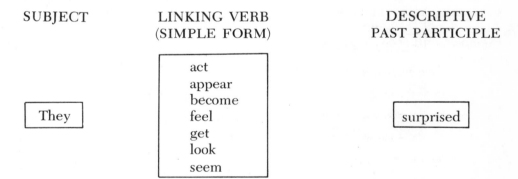

SUBJECT	LINKING VERB (SIMPLE FORM)	DESCRIPTIVE PAST PARTICIPLE
They	act appear become feel get look seem	surprised

Practice

Underline the linking verb in each sentence. Then circle the descriptive past participle that completes the sentence.

Examples: The window *was* (polish, (polished))
Nellie *seems* highly (qualify, (qualified)) for the job.

1. I am (please, pleased) when an audience enjoys my singing.

2. Jerry looks (hurry, hurried).

3. June gets (offended, offend) easily.

4. I always get (scare, scared) when I hear loud noises.

5. When I saw the spider, I was (horrify, horrified).

6. If we look (surprise, surprised) to see you, it's because we are!

7. Harry acts (married, marry).

8. Andy told me he felt very (depress, depressed) when he was alone.

9. My employer seems (prejudice, prejudiced).

10. The deer become (frighten, frightened) when cars approach the woods.

11. The teacher is truly (interested, interest) in our progress.

12. The man dropped his tray and looked (embarrass, embarrassed).

13. You look so (dignify, dignified) in that high silk hat.

14. My friend seemed (confused, confuse) when she heard the news.

15. That tree appears to be (petrify, petrified).

16. The freshmen are (involved, involve) in writing a play.

17. Marna always acted (bored, bore) at my parties, so I stopped inviting her.

18. These sweet potatoes look (candy, candied).

19. The camera lens is (scratch, scratched).

20. Did you know that one out of three American couples gets (divorce, divorced)?

21. Well, I'm the hopeful type; I just got (engaged, engage).

22. Were you ever (baptize, baptized)?

23. White sugar and white flour are (refine, refined).

24. The people are (concerned, concern) about the rising cost of living.

25. That new car looks well (design, designed).

PART H: Present and Past Tense Practice
(Linking Verbs + Past Participle)

| (1) John feels trapped. | (2) John felt trapped. |

○ What tense is sentence (1)? How do you know?
   What tense is sentence (2)? How do you know?

○ Sentence (1) is present tense because the linking verb *feels* is present tense. Changing *feels* to *felt* in (2) changes the whole sentence from present to past. The past participle *trapped* has nothing to do with tense.

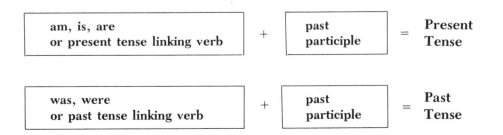

Practice   1

The sentences on the left below are present tense; those on the right, past tense. If the present tense is written on the left, write in the past tense on the line at the right, or vice versa.

Present Tense	**Past Tense**
Example: Smoking is forbidden.	*Smoking was forbidden.*

1. The lock seems broken.   1. _____

2. _____   2. We got finished early.

3. _____   3. I was surprised.

4. Tony feels determined to win.   4. _____

5. That store looks closed.   5. _____

6. _____   6. We were supposed to clean up.

7. The room is too crowded.   7. _____

8. They get used to prison life.   8. _____

9. _____   9. The cat was run over by a car.

10. _____   10. Sally was well dressed.

Practice   2

Below is a list of linking verbs and a list of main verbs. Make up ten sentences of your own in both present and past tense, combining a helping verb from column A and the past participle of a verb from column B.

A. Helpers-linkers   +   **B. Main verbs**

to be	to tire	to play
to act	to catch	to attach
to become	to involve	to teach
to get	to interest	to mix
to seem	to suppose	to force
to appear	to encourage	to bust
to feel	to threaten	
to look	to prepare	

Example:

Present: *Rhoda and I are involved in the women's movement.*
Past: *Rhoda and I were involved in the women's movement.*

1. Present: _____

   Past: _____

2. Present: _____

   Past: _____

3. Present: _____

   Past: _____

4. Present: _____

   Past: _____

5. Present: _____

   Past: _____

6. Present: _____

   Past: _____

7. Present: _____

   Past: _____

8. Present: _____

   Past: _____

9. Present: _____

   Past: _____

10. Present: _____

    Past: _____

PART I: Using Past Participles as Adjectives

(1) That broken window looks terrible.

(2) The lost child returned home today.

- ○ In (1) above, the verb is *looks*. Is there a past participle in the sentence?
- ○ *Broken* is the past participle of *to break*, but in (1) *broken* is not used with a helping verb. In fact, it is not a verb at all.
- ○ Instead, *broken* is an adjective describing the noun *window*.

○ What *participle* is used as an adjective, or a descriptive word, in (2)?

_____ (fill in) What word does it describe? _____ (fill in)

It is easy to see how the linking verb plus descriptive past participle (*The window is broken*) becomes past participle as adjective (*The broken window . . .*).

Practice 1

Use the past participles of the verbs listed below as adjectives. Use a different past participle to describe each noun.

Then, use your adjective-noun combination in a sentence.

to marry	to tire	to forget
to cut	to steal	to break
to polish	to dry	to speak
to fall	to misspell	to contaminate
to dread	to confuse	to civilize

Example: a *polished* apple

Example: A *polished apple tastes better than an unpolished one.*

1. two _____ windows

_____

2. a _____ child

_____

3. several _____ words

_____

4. the _____ man

_____

5. a _____ monster

_____

6. this _____ flower

_____

7. a _____ promise

_____

8. one _____ necklace

_____

9. some _____ athletes

_____

10. the _____ fruit

_____

Practice 2

Below are pairs of short sentences. Find and underline the past participle. Then rewrite each pair as **one** smooth sentence by using the past participle as an adjective.

Example: The book is lost. It is worth $1000.00.
  The lost book is worth $1000.00.

1. The envelope is sealed. John gave it to me.

_____

2. That man is distinquished. He always carried a cane.

_____

3. The woman is beautifully dressed. She roars by us on a motorbike.

_____

4. These apricots are dried. They are one health food that tastes delicious.

_____

5. The pavement is worn. It makes me imagine all the people who have passed here.

_____

6. This meat is chopped. Try it.

_____

7. The product is finished. It will please you, I am sure.

_____

8. The stones were cut and polished. An artisan set them in a gold ring.

_____

9. The living room was rearranged. It looks much better.

_____

10. The floor was newly stained. It smelled terrible.

_____

9

FIXED–FORM HELPING VERBS

PART A: Spotting and Defining the Fixed-form Helping Verb
PART B: Using the Fixed-form Helpers
PART C: Using CAN and COULD to Show Present and Past Tense
PART D: Using CAN and COULD to Show Certainty and Possibility
PART E: Using WILL and WOULD to Show Present and Past Tense
PART F: Using WILL and WOULD to Show Certainty and Possibility

PART A: Spotting and Defining the Fixed-form Helping Verbs

You already know the common—and changeable—helping verbs: *to have* and *to be*. Here are some unchanging helping verbs you should know:

The Fixed-form Helpers	
will	would
can	could
may	might
shall	should
must	

Practice

Write one fixed-form helping verb in each sentence below. Try to use all of them.

1. Your friends ＿＿＿＿＿ come if they want to.

2. Jennie ＿＿＿＿＿ ride a horse.

3. This jacket ＿＿＿＿＿ dry quickly.

4. I really _____ read this book more closely.

5. Who knows? We _____ adopt a child.

6. If I didn't know Herb so well, I _____ think he was crazy.

7. John _____ have gone home already.

8. It _____ rain this afternoon.

9. The yoga instructor said they _____ breathe more deeply.

10. You _____ graduate in the spring.

○ Do you see why these verbs are called fixed-form helpers?

○ Unlike other verbs, they do not change to agree with the subject of a sentence. They always keep the same form.

PART B: Using the Fixed-form Helpers

> (1) Al will stay with us this summer.

> (2) She can shoot a rifle well.

○ *Will* is the fixed-form helper in sentence (1). What main verb does it

   help? _____ (fill in)

○ *Can* is the fixed-form helper in (2). What main verb does it help?

   _____ (fill in)

○ Note that *stay* and *shoot* are the simple forms of the verbs.

When a verb has two parts—a fixed-form helping verb and a main verb—the main verb is in its simple form and does not show tense in any way.

Practice

In column A, each sentence contains a verb made up of some form of **to have** (changeable helping verb) and a **past participle** (main verb).

   In column B, each sentence contains a two-part verb made up of a fixed-form helping verb and a blank. Write in the correct form of the main verb.

Column A: Have + Past Participle   **Column B: Fixed-form Helper + Simple Form**

Examples: I have talked to him.   I may *talk* to him.
             She has taken so long.   She will *take* so long.

1. He has finished the painting.   1. He can _____ the painting.

2. The children have understood.

3. It has broken.

4. I have seen an eclipse.

5. She has decided to go.

6. We have sung the *Messiah*.

7. The Indians have given much.

8. They have gone now.

9. Have you used it all?

10. I have cherished that book.

2. The children should _____ .

3. It could _____ .

4. I might _____ an eclipse.

5. She may _____ to go.

6. We will _____ the *Messiah*.

7. The Indians could _____ much.

8. They will _____ now.

9. Must you _____ it all?

10. I shall _____ that book.

○ Did you remember to write only the simple forms of the main verbs in column B?

PART C: Using CAN and COULD to Show Present and Past Tense

(1) He says that I *can* use any tools in his garage.

(2) He said that I *could* use any tools in his garage.

○ What is the tense of sentence (1)? _____ (fill in)
○ What is the tense of sentence (2)? _____ (fill in)
○ What is the helping verb in (1)? _____ (fill in)
○ What is the helping verb in (2)? _____ (fill in)
○ As you can see, *could* may be used as the past tense of *can*.

Present tense: Today I *can* touch my toes.

Past tense: Yesterday I *could* touch my toes.

Can means am/is/are *able*. It can be used to show present tense.

Could means was/were *able* when it is used to show past tense of *can*.

Practice 1

Try these exercises. Fill in the present tense helper **can** or the past tense **could,** whichever is needed. Look at other verbs in each sentence to determine whether a sentence is present or past. Or, look for the time words like **now**, **yesterday**, etc.

1. As the noise outside my door stops, I _____ breathe again.

2. As the noise outside my door stopped, I _____ breathe again.

3. She says that she _____ swim.

4. She said that she _____ swim.

5. Last Friday I _____ not attend the concert.

6. Tonight I _____ not attend the concert.

7. When the guests leave, I _____ play my stereo.

8. When the guests left, I _____ play my stereo.

9. If he felt like it, Tony _____ cook a great meal.

10. If he feels like it, Tony _____ cook a great meal.

Practice 2

Circle either the present tense **can** or the past tense **could:**

1. You should meet Tony; he (can, could) lift a fifty pound weight.
2. I (can, could) never tell if Sharon was kidding or not.
3. When my father was a boy, you (can, could) buy a soda for a nickel.
4. When darkness falls out here, you (can, could) hear fish leaping in the water.
5. Yesterday I (could, can) not find the gym.
6. I hope you (can, could) come with us today.
7. It so happened that Hedda (can, could) not sleep on that fateful night.
8. You (can, could) do anything if you have a positive attitude.
9. Once we thought we (can, could) fly, so we took an umbrella to the roof.
10. Watch this; I (can, could) play the piano with my toes.

Practice 3

Now write three sentences using **can** to show present tense and three sentences using **could** to show past tense.

1. _____

2. _____

3. _____

4. _____

5. _____

6. _____

PART D: Using CAN and COULD to Show Certainty and Possibility

Besides showing present and past tense, these two fixed-form helpers can show another kind of difference.

> (1) Ruth *can* swim today.

> (2) Ethel *could* swim today if it weren't so cold.

- Who is more likely to swim today, Ruth or Ethel?
- *Ruth can swim* leaves no doubt. She is able to swim today; that is a fact. Ethel, on the other hand, *could* swim *but . . .* it is a possibility, perhaps even a wish; but it is not a fact.
- The difference between *can* and *could* here is not tense, but rather, *can* in sentence (1) shows a definite fact; *could* in sentence (2) is more *iffy*.

Can **means** *definitely able to do something.* **It shows a definite fact.**

Could **means** *might do something,* **if . . . . It shows possibility only.**

Practice   1

Write either **can** (definite) or **could** (possible) in the sentences below:

1. If I _____ carry a tune, I would sing with you.

2. Nora _____ cook Chinese food.

3. Julio thinks he _____ do anything better than you can.

4. If I _____ lend you the money, I would.

5. To achieve your dream, you must believe you _____ .

6. If only our class _____ go to Puerto Rico for the weekend!

7. That man _____ really dance.

8. It _____ be true, I just don't know.

9. Sam _____ do 50 push-ups.

10. I wish I _____ do as many.

11. If I had gone to college, I _____ have applied for the job.

12. If only spring _____ last all year long.

Practice 2

Write three sentences using **can** to show certainty and three sentences using **could** to show possibility.

1. _____

2. _____

3. _____

4. _____

5. _____

6. _____

PART E: Using WILL and WOULD to Show Present and Past Tense

> (1) You know you *will* do well in that class.

> (2) You knew you *would* do well in that class.

- ○ Sentence (1) says that *you know* now (present tense) that you *will* do well in the future. *Will* points to the future from the present.
- ○ Sentence (2) says that *you knew* then (past tense) that you *would* do well after that. *Would* points to the future from the past.
- ○ *Would* may be used as the past tense of *will*, just as *could* may be used as the past tense of *can*.

Practice 1

Fill in the present tense **will** or the past tense **would.**

1. Herb knows that he _____ win someday.

2. Herb knew that he _____ win someday.

3. If we arrived early, we _____ get the best seats.

4. If we arrive early, we _____ get the best seats.

5. If they have enough money left, they _____ hire a band.

6. If they had enough money left, they _____ hire a band.

7. We say we _____ have seven children.

8. We said we _____ have seven children.

9. I know that I _____ graduate with honors.

10. Last year I knew that I _____ graduate with honors.

Practice 2

Circle the present tense **will** or the past tense **would.**

1. He said he (will, would) help me whenever I needed help.

2. The students hope that they (will, would) all receive A's.

3. My history instructor promised us that he (will, would) grade the tests fairly.

4. The pants (will, would) fit when I lose weight.

5. They said they (will, would) visit, but they never did.

6. If you lend me money, I (will, would) buy that sweater.

7. The roast beef (will, would) burn unless you take it out of the oven.

8. Sally wondered what she (will, would) wear to the opera.

Practice 3

Write three sentences using **will** to show present tense and three sentences using **would** to show past tense.

1. _____

2. _____

3. _____

4. _____

5. _____

6. _____

PART F: Using WILL and WOULD to Show Certainty and Possibility

> (1) Charles *will* mow the lawn.

> (2) Ray *would* mow the lawn, but he doesn't feel very well.

○ Who do you bet will cut the grass, Charles or Ray?

○ Charles, of course, is a sure thing because he *will* mow the lawn, a definite statement of fact. Ray, on the other hand, *would* cut the grass, *but* . . . it is only a possibility, unlikely at that.

○ *Will* as used in (1) shows certain future action, definite fact. *Would* as used in (2) is more *iffy*, showing possibility, not fact; *would* shows a dream or wish with an *if* or *but* or *maybe* attached.

Practice 1

Write either **will** (definite) or **would** (possible) in each sentence below:

1. Grandma _____ wash the car tomorrow.

2. If I had a million dollars, I _____ buy a mink bathtub.

3. The Jacksons _____ move to Maine and fish for lobsters.

4. "How _____ you like a knuckle sandwich?" she asked him.

5. If I were you, I _____ not hang out the window like that.

6. We _____ like to visit Africa.

7. We _____ visit Africa.

8. If it weren't so cool, Jean _____ wear her sundress.

9. We must evacuate the ship because the tank _____ explode.

10. Sondra _____ write to us if she could.

11. They _____ have baked brownies if they knew you were coming.

12. I _____ phone you.

Practice 2

Write three sentences using **will** to show certainty and three sentences using **would** to show possibility.

1. _____

2. _____

3. _____

4. _____

5. _____

6. _____

10

PROGRESSIVE TENSES
(To Be + –ing Verb Form)

PART A: **Defining and Writing Present Progressive Tense**

PART B: **Defining and Writing Past Progressive Tense**

PART C: **Using the Progressive Tenses**

PART D: **Avoiding Incomplete Progressives**

PART A: **Defining and Writing Present Progressive Tense**

> (1) Roland *plays* tennis.

> (2) Roland *is playing* tennis.

○ What is the time of sentence (1)? What word tells you? _____

_____(fill in)

○ What is the time of sentence (2)? What word tells you? _____

_____(fill in)

○ The time of both sentences is present (even though they *mean* somewhat different things). In (1), *plays*, a present tense verb, gives present time to the sentence.

○ In (2), the verb has two parts: helping verb *is* + *playing*. By itself, *playing* has no time, so it is the present tense *is* that tells the time in (2).

Present Progressive Tense
(example verb: **to play**)

I am playing	we are playing
you are playing	you are playing
he ⎫	
she ⎬ is playing	they are playing
it ⎭	

103

Practice   1

Change each one-word present tense verb in the left-hand column to the two-part present progressive verb in the right-hand column. Do this by filling in the missing helping verb **(am, is,** or **are)**.

Present Tense	**Present Progressive Tense**
Examples: I swim. He wears my sweater.	I *am* swimming. He *is* wearing my sweater.

1. You write rapidly.

2. Irma and I shop downtown.

3. They sing.

4. My research begins to pay off.

5. We eat at six o'clock.

6. Joe works out at the gym.

7. Debbie hikes and runs.

8. You become popular.

9. Frank gets lazy.

10. You probably wonder why.

1. You _____ writing rapidly.

2. Irma and I _____ shopping downtown.

3. They _____ singing.

4. My research _____ beginning to pay off.

5. We _____ eating at six o'clock.

6. Joe _____ working out at the gym.

7. Debbie _____ hiking and running.

8. You _____ becoming popular.

9. Frank _____ getting lazy.

10. You _____ probably wondering why.

Remember: Every verb in present progressive tense must have two parts: helping verb and *-ing* main verb. The helping verb must agree with the subject.

Practice   2

Below are sentences in the regular present tense. Rewrite each one in present progressive tense by changing the verb to **am, is,** or **are + -ing form of the main verb.**

Example: We write letters.
            We are writing letters.

1. John and Norma date each other.

_____

2. Desmond tries too hard.

_____

3. The lakes freeze over.

_____

4. I keep a journal of thoughts and observations.

_____

5. After our last class, we go over to the pub for an hour or so.

_____

PART B: Defining and Writing Past Progressive Tense

| (1) Roland *played* tennis. | (2) Roland *was playing* tennis. |

○ What is the time of sentence (1)? What word tells you? _____ (fill in)

○ What is the time of sentence (2)? What word tells you? _____ (fill in)

○ Both (1) and (2) show past time. Past tense verb *played* shows past time in (1). In (2), the verb has two parts: helping verb *was* + *playing*. Past tense helper *was* gives past time to the two-part verb.

○ The verb *was playing* is past progressive tense.

Past Progressive Tense
(example verb: **to play**)

I was playing   we were playing
you were playing   you were playing
he ⎫
she ⎬ was playing   they were playing
it ⎭

Practice 1

Change each one-word past tense verb in the left-hand column to the two-part past progressive form in the right-hand column. Do this by filling in the missing helping verb (**was** or **were**).

Past Tense	**Past Progressive Tense**
Examples: I swam.	I *was* swimming.
He wore my sweater.	He *was* wearing my sweater.
1. You wrote rapidly.	1. You _____ writing rapidly.

2. Irma and I shopped downtown.

3. They sang.

4. My research began to pay off.

5. We ate at six o'clock.

6. Joe worked out at the gym.

7. Debbie hiked and ran.

8. You became popular.

9. Frank got lazy.

10. You probably wondered why.

2. Irma and I _____ shopping downtown

3. They _____ singing.

4. My research _____ beginning to pay off.

5. We _____ eating at six o'clock.

6. Joe _____ working out at the gym.

7. Debbie _____ hiking and running.

8. You _____ becoming popular.

9. Frank _____ getting lazy.

10. You _____ probably wondering why.

Practice 2

Below are sentences in the past tense. Rewrite each sentence in Past Progressive Tense by changing the verb to **was or were** + **-ing form of the main verb.**

Example: You cooked dinner.
            You were cooking dinner.

1. The two boys carried all the bookcases into the street.

   _____

2. We hoped the sun would shine today.

   _____

3. I did my best.

   _____

4. A cold wind blew all day.

   _____

5. He acted like a patient, not a doctor!

   _____

PART C: Using the Progressive Tenses

As you changed regular present and past tense verbs to the Progressive Present and Past Tense, did you hear the differences in meaning?

---

(1) Lenore *plays* the piano.

---

(2) Al *is playing* the piano.

---

o Which person is definitely at the keyboard right now?

o If you said Al, you are right. He *is* now *in the process of playing* the piano. Lenore, on the other hand, *does* play the piano; she may also paint, write novels, and play centerfield, but we do not know from the sentence what she *is doing now.*

o The Present Progressive verb *is playing* tells us that the action is *in progress.*

---

(1) Linda *washed* her hair every day.

---

(2) Linda *was washing* her hair when we arrived for the party.

---

o In (1) *washed* implies a daily, habitual action.

o The Past Progressive verb in (2) has a special meaning: that Linda was *in the process* of washing her hair when something else happened (we arrived).

o Note that to say "Linda *washed* her hair *when* we arrived for the party" means that first we arrived, and then Linda started washing her hair.

There is one more use of Progressive Tense that you probably already know:

Tony *is coming* over later.

---

o The Present Progressive verb *is coming* shows *future* time: Tony *is going to come* over.

In English, we use the Progressive Tenses *much less often* than regular present tense and past tense. We use the progressives only when we want to emphasize that something is or was in the process of happening.

Use *Present Progressive Tense* (am, is, are + -*ing*) to show that an action is in progress now or to show that an action is going to happen in the future.

Use *Past Progressive Tense* (was, were + -*ing*) to show that an action was in progress at a certain time in the past.

Practice

Read each sentence carefully for meaning. Then circle the verb that best expresses the meaning of the sentence.

Example: Right now we (write, (are writing)) letters.

1. Where is Tony? He (reads, is reading) in his room.
2. Donald (has, is having) a scholarship this year.
3. His sister (had, was having) a scholarship last year.
4. It was icy yesterday and my uncle (fell, was falling) down.
5. Music usually (soothes, is soothing) my nerves.
6. My dog Gourmand (eats, is eating) anything at all!
7. At this very moment, Gourmand (eats, is eating) the sports page.
8. That strange man (winked, was winking) once, then ran.
9. Helene (believes, is believing) in witchcraft.
10. We (watched, were watching) TV when there was a knock at the door.
11. When I was a child in the South, we (went, were going) to church every Sunday.
12. That teacher (knows, is knowing) how to keep a class interested.
13. What does Felix do best? He (plays, is playing) the saxophone.
14. I (go, am going) to Bolivia next year.
15. A woman of many interests, she (flies, is flying) planes and (reads, is reading) a book a day.
16. Stan (found, was finding) just what he was looking for in an army surplus store.
17. Phil (took, was taking) a bath when his friends stopped by.
18. Look! Jessica (talks, is talking) to herself!
19. As soon as I finish this work, I (take, am taking) a break.
20. Bakar (gave, was giving) his speech when the lights in the auditorium went out.
21. Most mornings we (get, are getting) up at 6 a.m.
22. Please don't bother me now; I (study, am studying).
23. She (broke, was breaking) her arm last year.
24. Jane said that she (comes, is coming) over tonight.

PART D: Avoiding Incomplete Progressives

Now that you can write both present and past progressive verbs, here is a mistake you should not make:

We having fun. *(incomplete)*

○ Can you see what is missing?

○ All by itself the *-ing* form *having* is not a verb. It has to have a helper.

○ Because the helping verb is missing, *we having fun* has no time! It could mean *we are having fun* or *we were having fun*.

○ *We having fun* is not a sentence, but a fragment of a sentence.

Practice   1

Each group of words below is incomplete. Read each group and put an X over the exact spot where a word is missing.

In Column A, write the word that would complete the sentence in *Present Progressive Tense.*

In Column B, write the word that would complete the sentence in *Past Progressive Tense.*

	A Present Progressive	B Past Progressive
Example: He ˣ having fun.	*is* (He is having fun.)	*was* (He was having fun.)
1. Maria always talking on the telephone.	_____	_____
2. People laughing and joking around.	_____	_____
3. George having trouble with his in-laws.	_____	_____
4. We playing baseball tonight.	_____	_____
5. Julio coming to my place after the game.	_____	_____
6. You studying botany and zoology.	_____	_____
7. After the third act, we going home.	_____	_____
8. Fights about money getting me down.	_____	_____
9. Joe and Pete both sitting on the curb.	_____	_____
10. The wind howling.	_____	_____
11. You going out too much lately.	_____	_____
12. My next door neighbor always drag racing in my driveway.	_____	_____
13. The leaves falling to the ground.	_____	_____
14. We all flying the helicopter downtown to the hamburger shack.	_____	_____

Practice 2

Read through this paragraph for incomplete progressive verbs. Then rewrite the entire paragraph on the lines below, completing any incomplete verbs.

It was a cold and lonely night at sea. The wind howling and waves groaning in the dark. We sitting on deck, smoking and thinking of home. I wanted to write down my feelings, but the words refusing to come. My paper staring back at me as lonely and blank as the stars.

Rewrite: _____

_____

_____

_____

_____

_____

11

CO-ORDINATION

PART A: Defining Co-ordinating Conjunctions
PART B: Correcting Run-ons and Comma Splices

PART A: Defining Co-ordinating Conjunctions

Read these sentences:

(1) First she is going to the bookstore to purchase her texts, and then she hopes to go to the movies.

(2) He wanted to get all A's, but he couldn't get more than a B in psychology.

(3) Wear rubbers in a heavy rain, for it is easy to catch cold in bad weather.

(4) Do your homework slowly and carefully, or you will have trouble with the work in class tomorrow.

- Can you break the first sentence above into two complete and independent ideas or thoughts? What are they? Underline the subject and verb in each.

- Can you do the same with the second and third and fourth? Underline subject and verb.

- In each sentence, circle the word that joins the two parts of the sentence together. What mark of punctuation precedes that word?

○ *And, but, for,* and *or* are co-ordinating conjunctions because they can conjoin (join) ideas together.

To join two complete and independent ideas together, use *and, but, for,* or *or* preceded by a comma.

Now that you know what co-ordinating conjunctions do, it might be a good idea to review exactly *how* they connect ideas.

(1)   He always has a ball at parties,

and

everybody loves to invite him.

In sentence (1), *and* joins the two ideas together. It acts like a plus sign (+).

(2)   She is always a sore loser,

but

everyone likes her anyway.

In sentence (2), *but* shows opposition. *But* forces you to contrast the two ideas. You might expect people not to like her because she is a sore loser, *but* (what a surprise!) they do like her anyway.

(3)   Don't ride your bike at night without lights,

for

you may have an accident.

In sentence (3), *for* introduces a reason. The second thought tells you why you should not ride at night without lights.

(4)   Do everything neatly and correctly,

or

don't bother to do it at all.

In sentence (4), there is a choice. *Or* says you can do this *or* you can do that. Pick one, not both. A choice.

and = addition
but = opposition
for = reason
or = choice

Practice   1

Fill in the correct co-ordinating conjunction between the complete and independent thoughts. Remember: do you want to add, oppose, give a reason, or indicate a choice?

1. He never comes to class on time, _____ *but* he always passes with A's.

2. The lamp never seems to work correctly, _____ *and* the television is on the blink too.

3. I will go to medical school and become a doctor, _____ *or* I will go to law school and become a lawyer.

4. You should never sit on that chair, _____ *for* it is an antique and might break easily.

5. This exercise wasn't that difficult, _____ *but* it took me almost two hours to do it.

6. Hedda had to drive all the way to Toronto, Canada, _____ *for* she was unable to get an airline ticket.

7. The bureau drawer has to be repaired, _____ *or* we will have to throw it out.

8. These shoes cost more than what I had expected to pay, _____ *but* they are worth the price, _____ *but* I think that I will treat myself and buy them.

9. This assignment was fun to do, _____ *and* I learned a great deal from it.

10. I guess I will have to wear my red suit, _____ *but* I'm not happy about it.

11. Enrollment in college has gone up in the past ten years, _____ *for* more and more people feel the need for higher education.

12. Her saxophone cost $200, _____ *but* the tone isn't very good.

Practice 2

Every one of these thoughts is complete by itself, but you can add two of them together to make more interesting sentences. Using **and, but, for,** or **or,** combine pairs of these thoughts and write 6 new sentences on the lines below. Punctuate correctly.

- they are the best pool players on the block
- Sonia is the greatest when it comes to guitar
- show some respect for the older people in the room
- John is dynamite in mathematics
- you will have to leave
- Doris has always wanted to be a lawyer
- they can't beat my cousin from Detroit
- she is utterly fantastic on piano
- it was raining hard and he had no umbrella
- he is going to apply for a scholarship
- he decided not to stay home and watch television
- discrimination against women has not undermined her plans

1. _____

2. _____

3. _____

4. _____

5. _____

6. _____

Practice 3

Finish these sentences by adding **a second complete idea** after the co-ordinating conjunction.

1. I never play baseball on Saturday, but _____

   _____

2. She hopes to graduate this semester, and _____

   _____

3. Keep your trap shut, or _____

   _____

4. I don't think I can trust him any longer, for _____

   _____

5. The bureau is the nicest piece of furniture I have, and _____

   _____

6. I will go shopping tomorrow, or _____

   _____

7. Maria speaks Spanish to her father, but _____

   _____

8. The classes are being held on the tennis courts, for _____

   _____

9. I love animals, but _____

   _____

10. I love animals, for _____

    _____

Practice 4

Here is a little story with the story left out. The sentence patterns are shown, but you fill in the story.

I went _____ , and he _____

_____ . He never _____ , but this

time he _____

_____ . His friend said _____

_____ , for she _____

_____ . After all, he _____

_____ , or _____ .

PART B: Correcting Run-ons and Comma Splices

Now that you know how to join ideas together with co-ordinating conjunctions, here are two problems to avoid.

1. RUN-ON

The air is filled with the sound of birds the grass is a beautiful shade of green.

2. COMMA SPLICE

The air is filled with the sound of birds, the grass is a beautiful shade of green.

- ○ Note that both the *run-on* and the *comma splice* contain two complete and independent ideas.
- ○ The *run-on* has no *conjunction* to join the ideas together.
- ○ The *comma splice* has only a *comma* to join the ideas together (but no conjunction).

  Use a co-ordinating conjunction and a comma to join together two complete and independent ideas.

3. CORRECTED

The air is filled with the sound of birds, and the grass is a beautiful shade of green.

Practice

Correct these run-ons and comma splices.

1. The books are on the table near the window I don't know where the papers are.

2. The cat drank her milk noisily the dog just gulped down his raw meat.

3. I will go to Canada this summer I want to hike in the mountains.

4. She made that dress from a pattern she can't sew a button to save her soul.

5. The table will have to go near the piano we have to rearrange the whole room.

6. He always makes the baseball team this year his bad leg kept him on the bench most of the time.

7. This was the best movie I have ever seen I am glad I saw it.

8. She was the best student in her class naturally she got the highest grade.

9. He's going to medical school his lifelong ambition is to be a doctor.

10. The piano is terribly out of tune I can't stand to listen to it any longer.

11. He is always late for parties, no one seems to mind.

12. The chairs are too large for the room, the table looks awkward in the corner.

13. The washing machine blows bubbles all over the room, I would prefer that you don't use it.

14. I find history an interesting subject at school, it gives a good idea of what mankind has been doing for the past 3,000 years.

15. You must take the dog out for a walk every night, we will have to get rid of him.

16. I usually love apple pie the green mold on this one makes me think twice.

17. He is extremely careful about his footnotes he loves to get A's on his term papers.

18. The door makes a strange creaking noise it's beginning to make me nervous.

19. The phone has been ringing for the past hour no one seems to want to answer it.

20. I have put a new roof on the house this will be a very wet winter.

21. My old girl friend went back to school to become a lawyer everyone is proud of her.

22. The gym is just around the corner I never get around to going there.

23. That orange feathered hat is a bit too big I'll buy it anyway.

24. The tuxedo will have to be altered I'll have to get married in my shorts.

25. Sunshine is good for you too much sun is bad for you.

12
SUBORDINATION

PART A: Defining Subordinating Conjunctions
PART B: Using Subordinating Conjunctions
PART C: Punctuating Subordinating Conjunctions

PART A: Defining Subordinating Conjunctions

> He left the party early. It was no fun at all. He was walking down the street toward the subway. He met his first girl friend. They hadn't seen each other for a long time. They almost didn't recognize each other. A few seconds passed. He wanted to speak with her. He didn't know what to say. More long seconds passed. He took her hand in his.

This could have been the beginning of a good story, but notice how dull the writing is because the sentences are short and choppy.

Here is the same paragraph rewritten to make it more interesting.

> He left the party early *because* it was no fun at all. *As* he was walking down the street toward the subway, he met his first girl friend. *Since* they hadn't seen each other for a long time, they almost didn't recognize each other. A few seconds passed. He wanted to speak with her *although* he didn't know what to say. *After* more long seconds passed, he took her hand in his.

Notice that the paragraph now reads more smoothly and is more interesting because these words were added to it:

>> *because*
>> *as*
>> *since*
>> *although*
>> *after*

Because, as, since, although, and *after* are part of a large group of words called *subordinating conjunctions.* As you see from the paragraph, as conjunctions they join together ideas. But you must be careful when you use them because once you add them to an idea, that idea can no longer stand alone as a complete and independent sentence. It has become a subordinate (dependent) idea; it relies upon another idea to complete its meaning.

    a) Because he is tired . . .
    b) As I left the room . . .
    c) Since it is late . . .
    d) Although they are smart . . .
    e) After the class ended . . .

Notice that all of these ideas have to be followed by something else—another thought.

    a) Because he is tired, *he won't go.*

Complete these ideas:

    b) As I left the room, _____ .

    c) Since it is late, _____ .

    d) Although they are smart, _____ .

    e) After the class ended, _____ .

Here is list of some subordinating conjunctions (though not all of them):

after	if
although	since
as	when (ever)
as if	while
because	until

PART B: Using Subordinating Conjunctions

Practice   1

Read these sentences carefully for meaning; then write an appropriate subordinating conjunction in the blank space.

    1. _____ he played basketball last week, he hurt his knee.

    2. We left her house _____ the snow piled up six inches high.

    3. _____ he usually does well in science, he had trouble with biology.

    4. She acts _____ she were a queen.

5. _____ he was doing his homework, his friends went on a picnic.

6. I don't think I'll go _____ none of my close relatives will be there.

7. _____ I were you, I wouldn't do that.

8. _____ Pam jogs in the morning, she feels great all day long.

Practice 2

Now that you understand how subordinating conjunctions join thoughts together, try these sentences. Here you have to supply one idea. Make sure the ideas you add in the blank space have subjects and verbs.

1. Because Jose is from Puerto Rico, _____ .

2. If _____ , I'll scream.

3. After _____ , Robert and I went swimming in the pool.

4. Whenever _____ , he gets a severe headache.

5. I was washing stacks of dirty dishes while _____ .

6. Since it is Halloween, _____ .

7. He is an excellent carpenter although _____ .

8. Because the weather is uncomfortable, _____ .

9. As he gripped the revolver, _____ .

10. He visits his parents whenever _____ .

Practice 3

These exercises require you to work harder. Here you have to supply both ideas. Make sure both thoughts are complete.

Example: When *he left the room,* *the light went on.*

1. After _____ , _____ .

2. Since _____ , _____ .

3. _____ because _____ .

4. _____ while _____ .

5. If _____ , _____ .

6. _____ as _____ .

7. Whereas _____ , _____ .

8. Because _____ , _____ .

9. _____ whenever _____ .

10. Although _____ , _____ .

Practice 4

Here is a little story—with the story left out. The subordinating conjunctions are there, but **you** have to fill in everything else.

When Bob _____ , he _____ .

He _____ after he _____

_____ . Later that day _____

_____ . While Bob _____

_____ , he _____

_____ . He _____ because

_____ .

He decided to _____

_____ . Although he _____

_____ , _____

_____ .

PART C: Punctuating Subordinating Conjunctions

As you may have noticed in the preceding exercises, some sentences with subordinating conjunctions used a comma and others did not. Here is how it's done:

<table>
<tr><td align="center">(1)</td><td align="center">(2)</td></tr>
<tr><td>Because it rained very hard, we had to leave early.</td><td>We had to leave early because it rained very hard.</td></tr>
</table>

○ Sentence (1) has a comma because the subordinate idea precedes the main idea.

<table>
<tr><td>Because it rained very hard</td><td>,</td><td>we had to leave early.</td></tr>
<tr><td align="center">subordinate idea</td><td align="center">,</td><td align="center">main idea</td></tr>
</table>

o Sentence (2) has no comma because the subordinate idea follows the main idea.

| We had to leave early | because it rained very hard. |

      main idea   *subordinate idea*

Use a comma after a subordinate idea; do not use a comma before a subordinate idea.

Practice

Here are some skeleton sentences. The subordinate ideas begin with a subordinating conjunction. Fill in the blanks, being careful to **use the comma** when necessary. **Do not use the comma** when the main idea precedes the subordinate idea.

1. _____ because
_____ .

2. Although _____
_____ .

3. Since _____
_____ .

4. _____ whenever _____
_____ .

5. If _____
_____ .

6. _____ while _____
_____ .

7. As _____
_____ .

8. _____ because _____
_____ .

13
SEMI-COLON

So far you have learned to join ideas together in two ways:

   o co-ordinating conjunctions
    (and, but, for, or, etc.)

        | or |

   o subordinating conjunctions
    (although, because, as, etc.)

> (1) This is the worst food we have ever tasted.

> (2) We will never eat at this restaurant again.

How would you join ideas (1) and (2) together?

   o with a co-ordinating conjunction

(1) _____ , and

(2) _____ .

   o with a subordinating conjunction:

(1) Because _____ ,

(2) _____ .

   o Here is another way to join ideas:

(1) _____ ;

(2) _____ .

A *semi-colon* can join two independent ideas without a conjunction:

> *This is the worst food we have ever tasted;*
> *we will never eat at this restaurant again.*

Do not capitalize the first word after the semi-colon.

Practice 1

Each independent idea below is the first half of a sentence. Add a semi-colon and a second complete idea. Make sure that your second thought is also independent and can stand alone.

1. The kids roller skate around the block _____

   _____

2. These books are fascinating reading for sailors _____

   _____

3. In the afternoon, the gardener watered the flowers _____

   _____

4. She travels around the country playing piano professionally _____

   _____

5. Some students prefer not to write term papers _____

   _____

6. The red lamp in the corner is an antique _____

   _____

7. Puerto Rico is one of the most beautiful islands in the Caribbean _____

   _____

8. Paul has been on a diet for three months _____

   _____

9. Sylvia talks to her house plants _____

   _____

10. Reading books and magazines, Bill keeps up with the latest in photography _____

    _____

BE CAREFUL: *Do not* use a semi-colon between a subordinate idea and an independent idea.

> Although he is never at home, he is not difficult to reach elsewhere.

- You cannot use a semi-colon in this sentence because the first idea (*although he is never at home*) cannot stand alone.
- The word *although* requires that the idea be joined to a complete idea with a comma.

Practice   2

Which of these ideas can be followed by a **semi-colon** and an independent thought? Check them (√).

1. The crowd of children played baseball all day ＿＿＿

2. Since the sun has already set ＿＿＿

3. As he was riding to school ＿＿＿

4. While I do my homework, Sara plays ＿＿＿

5. My shopping bag is so full it is ready to burst ＿＿＿

6. While I do the dishes ＿＿＿

Now re-copy the sentences you have checked; add a semi-colon and complete the sentence with a second independent idea. You should have checked sentences (1), (4) and (5).

＿＿＿＿＿＿＿＿＿＿＿＿＿＿＿＿＿＿＿＿＿＿＿＿＿＿＿＿＿＿＿＿＿＿＿

＿＿＿＿＿＿＿＿＿＿＿＿＿＿＿＿＿＿＿＿＿＿＿＿＿＿＿＿＿＿＿＿＿＿＿

＿＿＿＿＿＿＿＿＿＿＿＿＿＿＿＿＿＿＿＿＿＿＿＿＿＿＿＿＿＿＿＿＿＿＿

＿＿＿＿＿＿＿＿＿＿＿＿＿＿＿＿＿＿＿＿＿＿＿＿＿＿＿＿＿＿＿＿＿＿＿

＿＿＿＿＿＿＿＿＿＿＿＿＿＿＿＿＿＿＿＿＿＿＿＿＿＿＿＿＿＿＿＿＿＿＿

＿＿＿＿＿＿＿＿＿＿＿＿＿＿＿＿＿＿＿＿＿＿＿＿＿＿＿＿＿＿＿＿＿＿＿

Practice   3

Here are blanks for you to fill in with ideas before and after the semi-colon. Make sure your thoughts are independent.

1. ＿＿＿＿＿＿＿＿＿＿＿＿＿＿＿＿＿＿＿＿＿＿＿＿＿＿ ; ＿＿＿＿＿＿＿

＿＿＿＿＿＿＿＿＿＿＿＿＿＿＿＿＿＿＿＿＿＿＿＿＿＿＿＿＿＿＿＿＿＿＿

2. _____

_____ ; _____

3. _____ ;

_____

4. _____

_____ ; _____

5. _____ ; _____

_____

14

ADVERBIAL CONJUNCTIONS

PART A: **Defining and Using Adverbial Conjunctions**

PART B: **Punctuating Adverbial Conjunctions**

PART A: Defining and Using Adverbial Conjunctions

This lesson will give you another method of joining ideas—by using a special kind of a *conjunction* and a *semi-colon*.

This special kind of *conjunction* is called an *adverbial conjunction* because it is part *adverb* and part *conjunction*.

Here is a basic list (though not a complete one) of *adverbial conjunctions:*

> **however**
> **moreover**
> **therefore**
> **nevertheless**

(1) (a) My pet cat washes herself every day; *however,*
     (b) she still has a funny smell.

○ *However* contrasts ideas (a) and (b).

○ The sentence might have been written, "My pet cat washes herself every day, *but* she still has a funny smell."

○ But the *however* is stronger, more emphatic.

○ Note the punctuation.

(2) (a) He received an A on his term paper; *moreover,*
     (b) the instructor exempted him from the final.

○ *Moreover* adds idea (b) to idea (a).

○ The sentence might have been written, "He received an A on his term paper, *and* the instructor exempted him from the final."

○ But the *moreover* is stronger, more emphatic.

○ Note the punctuation.

---

(3) (a) The complete dictionary weighs 30 pounds; *therefore,*
     (b) I bring my pocket edition to school.

○ *Therefore* shows that idea (a) is the cause of idea (b).

○ The sentence might have been written, "*Because* the complete dictionary weighs 30 pounds, I bring my pocket edition to school."

○ But the *therefore* is stronger, more emphatic.

○ Note the punctuation.

---

(4) (a) He rarely seems to study; *nevertheless,*
     (b) he always gets A's.

○ *Nevertheless* shows that idea (b) is true in spite of idea (a).

○ The sentence might have been written, "*Even though* he rarely seems to study, he always gets A's."

○ But *nevertheless* is stronger, more emphatic.

○ Note the punctuation.

An *adverbial conjunction* joins ideas together in an *emphatic* way. It may be used with a semi-colon only when both ideas are independent and can stand alone.

Practice

Add an idea after the adverbial conjunction. Keep in mind what **however, moreover, therefore** and **nevelreless** mean. The idea you add must make sense in terms of the entire sentence.

Example: I hate eating asparagus when I have a sore throat; **however,** *I love ice cream any time at all.*

1. My dog has trouble learning to do new tricks; **nevertheless,** _____

_____

_____

2. Getting a degree can involve a lot of work; **however,** _____

_____

_____

3. She received her law degree when she was 23 years old; **moreover,** _____

    _____

    _____

4. He found the trumpet an impossibly difficult instrument to play; **therefore,** _____

    _____

5. The white mice in the cage seem nervous; **however,** _____

    _____

6. The natives in the midst of the jungle do not have television sets; **nevertheless,** __

    _____

7. I haven't had any heat for a month; **therefore,** _____

    _____

8. Her paintings sell for a lot of money; **moreover** _____

    _____

PART B: Punctuating Adverbial Conjunctions

Note the punctuation pattern:

---
complete idea (a); adverbial conjunction, complete idea (b)

○ The adverbial conjunction is preceded by a semi-colon.
○ It is followed by a comma.

Practice   1

Punctuate these sentences.

1. Diet pills are often addictive however many people still take them.

2. I have trouble understanding French when it is spoken nevertheless I can read it quite easily.

3. Swimming is a good way to help you stop smoking moreover it is good exercise for your health in general.

4. The piano was much larger than I had realized therefore we had to move it into the other room.

5. My telephone has been out of order for weeks nevertheless people seem to be able to get in touch with me anyway.

6. Making clay pots is a marvelous hobby moreover it is not as difficult as most people think.

7. Sam types twenty-five or thirty letters a day however he really hates doing office work.

8. She has a terrible fear of heights therefore I doubt that she will decide to become a window washer.

Practice 2

Add an adverbial conjunction **and** a second independent idea to each idea below. Then punctuate the entire sentence correctly.

1. Mexican food is quite spicy _____

_____

2. Many evening students must work all day _____

_____

3. The uprising at Attica called attention to prison conditions in America _____

_____

4. Herbal teas are not only delicious but good for you _____

_____

BE CAREFUL:

(1) *However,* I don't like him.

(2) I don't, *however,* like him.

(3) I don't like him, *however.*

○ Why aren't semi-colons used in sentences (1), (2), and (3)?

(4) If I were you, *however,* I would never talk to him again.

○ Are the two ideas of sentence (4) independent?
○ Never use a semi-colon to join if one of the ideas is subordinate.

Practice   3

Write eight sentences, using **however** in two, **moreover** in two, **therefore** in two, and **nevertheless** in two. Make sure your ideas are independent. Be careful of the punctuation.

1. _____

   _____

2. _____

   _____

3. _____

   _____

4. _____

   _____

5. _____

   _____

6. _____

   _____

7. _____

   _____

8. _____

   _____

15
RELATIVES

PART A: **Defining the Relative**
PART B: **Combining Ideas with Relatives**
PART C: **Punctuating Relatives**

PART A: Defining the Relative*

> (1) My father is 80 years old.

> (2) He collects stamps.

- Sentences (1) and (2) are grammatically correct.
- But it is often good to join together related ideas, especially when they are as short and choppy as (1) and (2).

> (3) My father, who is 80 years old, collects stamps.

- Sentence (3) is a combination of (1) and (2).
- *Who* joins the ideas together.
- *Who* is called a *relative* because it *relates* "is 80 years old" to "my father."

   Here are some more examples of combinations:

> (1) He gives great singing lessons.

---

*For work on subject-verb agreement in relatives, see Chapter 6, Part G.

> (2) All his pupils love them.

> (3) He gives great singing lessons, *which* all his pupils love.

> (1) I have a large living room.

> (2) It can hold two grand pianos.

> (3) I have a large living room *that* can hold two grand pianos.

○ As you can see, *which* and *that* may also be used as relatives.

○ In the sentences above,

what does *which* relate or refer to? _____ (fill in);

what does *that* relate or refer to? _____ (fill in).

Who, *which*, or *that* as a relative always comes directly after the words it relates to.

My father, who is . . .
. . . lessons, which all . . .
. . . room that can . . .

PART B: Combining Ideas with Relatives

You now know that you can use *who, that* and *which* as relatives to join ideas together.

But *who, that* and *which* cannot be used interchangeably.

Who **refers to people.**
That **refers to people and/or things.**
Which **refers to things.**

Practice

Combine each set of sentences into one sentence. Make sure to use **who, which,** and **that** correctly.

Example:

1. The garden is beginning to sprout.

2. I planted it last week.

Combination: *The garden that I planted last week is beginning to sprout.*

1. Bill knows the material very well.

2. He expects to get an A.

Combination: _____

_____

1. I just bought a stereo.

2. It plays records at 4 speeds.

Combination: _____

_____

1. My rent is now $300 a month.

2. My rent is going up next month.

Combination: _____

_____

1. I just bought some cheese.

2. It looks delicious.

Combination: _____

_____

1. My mother couldn't find the flashlight.

2. She has bad eyesight.

Combination: _____

_____

1. My uncle has offered to teach me to use oil paints.

2. He is a fine painter.

Combination: _____

_____

1. I will buy this purple hat.

2. It looks wonderful on me.

Combination: _____

_____

1. My biology professor was the best teacher I ever had.

2. She never forgot that students are human beings.

Combination: _____

_____

1. Dancing is my favorite pastime.
2. It relaxes me after a long day of studying.

Combination: _____

_____

1. Henry caught a trout.
2. It was the largest fish ever recorded in Idaho.

Combination: _____

_____

PART C: Punctuating Relatives

RESTRICTIVE

> (1) Never eat peaches *that are green.*

- In sentence (1), the relative is _____ . (fill in)
- Can you leave out the relative *(that are green)* and still keep the basic meaning of the sentence?
- *No!* You are not saying *don't eat peaches* but *don't eat* certain kinds of peaches—*green* ones.
- Therefore, *that are green* is called *restrictive* because it *restricts* the meaning of the sentence.
- *Commas do not set off a restrictive relative.*

NONRESTRICTIVE

> (2) My guitar, *which is a Martin,* was given to me as a gift.

- In sentence (2), the relative is _____ . (fill in)
- Can you leave out the relative *(which is a Martin)* and still keep the basic meaning of the sentence?
- *Yes! Which is a Martin* merely adds a fact, but does not change the basic idea of the sentence, that *my guitar was given to me as a gift.*
- Therefore, *which is a Martin* is called *nonrestrictive* because it does not restrict or change the meaning of the sentence.
- *Use commas to set off a nonrestrictive relative.*

Nonrestrictive relatives **are set off by commas.** *Restrictive relatives* **require no punctuation.**

Practice 1

Punctuate these sentences correctly. A clue: **which** is usually used as a nonrestrictive relative.

1. Swimming which is good exercise is a lot of fun.

2. People who need people are the luckiest people in the world.

3. He loves books that can be read quickly.

4. Students who keep up with the homework usually do well on the final.

5. I always get stuck with clothing that goes out of style quickly.

6. This plant which is a rare one doesn't grow well indoors.

7. A person who gets angry easily may have few close friends.

8. I can't find the ruler that I just laid on my desk.

9. Elfrieda who has been my best friend for years has just decided to marry and leave the city.

10. Exercise that causes severe exhaustion is dangerous.

Practice 2

Write five sentences using nonrestrictive relatives and five using restrictive relatives. Be careful of your punctuation.

Nonrestrictive

1. _____

2. _____

3. _____

4. _____

5. _____

Restrictive

1. _____

2. _____

3. _____

4. _____

5. _____

16

–ING MODIFIERS

PART A: Using -ING Modifiers
PART B: Avoiding Confusing Modifiers

PART A: Using -ING Modifiers

> (1) Beth was learning to ski. She broke her ankle.

> (2) Learning to ski, Beth broke her ankle.

- It seems that *while* Beth was learning to ski, she had an accident. Sentence (2) emphasizes the relationship *and* joins two short sentences in one longer one.
- Remember that in (2), without its helper *was, learning* is no longer a verb. Instead, *learning to ski* refers to or modifies *Beth*, the subject of the new sentence.

> Learning to ski, Beth broke her ankle.

Practice

Combine the two repetitious sentences in each pair below by using the *-ing* modifier to connect them. Drop unnecessary words. Draw an arrow from the *-ing* word to the word it refers to.

Examples: Tom stood on the deck. He was drinking champagne.

  Drinking champagne, Tom stood on the deck.

We saw Emily. We were riding horses.

Riding horses, we saw Emily.

1. I was walking on the shore. I found some interesting shells.

   _____

2. The children were leaving school early. They spotted their friends.

   _____

3. Herb was singing in the shower. He woke the neighbors.

   _____

4. The friends were running on the moonlit beach. They felt close to nature and each other.

   _____

5. Bob and Mike were caught by the principal himself. They were smoking in the boys' room.

   _____

6. You are exploring an old house. You find a trunk filled with pearls and bubble gum.

   _____

7. Tom is doing research in the library. He often makes exciting discoveries there.

   _____

8. Scientists are tagging sea birds. They hope to study flock movements.

   _____

9. Linda was swinging her arms and shrieking. She said it was her Kung Fu imitation.

   _____

10. The student senators enjoyed the evening together. They were listening to classical guitar and eating grapes.

    _____

PART B: Avoiding Confusing Modifiers

Be sure that your *-ing* modifiers say what you mean!

> (1) Hanging by the toe from the dresser drawer, Joe found his sock.

- Probably the writer did not mean that Joe spent time hanging by his toes. *What then was hanging by the toe from the dresser drawer?*
- *Hanging* refers to *sock* of course, but the order of the sentence does not show this. We could clear up the confusion by turning the ideas around.

> Joe found his sock hanging by the toe from the dresser drawer.

Read your sentences in the previous exercise to make sure the order of ideas is clear, not confusing.

> (2) Visiting my cousin, our house was robbed.

○ Does the writer mean here that *our house* was visiting my cousin? Who or what, then, does *visiting my cousin* refer to?

○ *Visiting* seems to refer to *I* but there is no *I* in the sentence. To clear up the confusion, we would have to add or change words.

> Visiting my cousin, I learned that our house was robbed.

Practice   1

Complete the following sentences by adding an idea after the **-ing** modifier. Make sure the meaning is clear.

1. Walking down the street, _____

   _____

2. Helping me with my French, _____

   _____

3. While playing first base, _____

   _____

4. Burning his hand on the oven, _____

   _____

5. Raising her champagne glass in a toast, _____

   _____

6. After digging for clams, _____

   _____

7. Jumping from the Empire State Building with a parachute, _____

   _____

8. Hoping to meet his girl friend in Acapulco, _____

    _____

9. Putting on her skis, _____

    _____

10. Polishing the furniture, _____

    _____

Practice 2

Write ten sentences of your own, using *-ing* modifiers to join ideas.

1. _____

2. _____

3. _____

4. _____

5. _____

6. _____

7. _____

8. _____

9. _____

10. _____

UNIT IV
NOUNS &
PRONOUNS
& OTHERS

17
NOUNS
(Singular and Plural)

PART A: Defining Singular and Plural
PART B: Making Nouns Plural
PART C: Signal Words: Singular
PART D: Signal Words: Plural
PART E: Signal Words with OF

PART A: Defining Singular and Plural

SINGULAR MEANS ONE

a boy
girl   } one of something
a student

PLURAL MEANS MORE THAN ONE

the boys
the girls   } more than one
the students

Practice

Write an "S" after the nouns that are singular; write a "P" after the nouns that are plural.

1. bookcase _____   4. desk _____

2. pen _____   5. wall _____

3. pencils _____   6. test _____

7. tables _____   9. pigeon _____

8. walls _____   10. holes _____

PART B: Making Nouns Plural

In the preceding practice, how did you know which nouns were singular (S) and which were plural (P)?

Write *your rule* here: _____

_____

_____

_____

      Yes, **nouns ending in** *-s* **are usually plural.**

Practice   1

Make these nouns into the plural.

Singular	**Plural**
1. clip	_____
2. hair	_____
3. rope	_____
4. belt	_____
5. dean	_____
6. student	_____
7. typist	_____
8. poster	_____

    ○ *A few nouns* form their plurals in other ways; here is a partial list:

Singular	**Plural**
mouse	mice
woman	women
man	men
child	child**ren**
goose	geese

○ *Others* do not change at all to form the plural; here is a partial list.

Singular	Plural
sheep	sheep
fish	fish
deer	deer
moose	moose

○ If you are ever unsure about the plural of a noun, check a dictionary.

Practice 2

Make these nouns plural.

Singular	Plural		Singular	Plural
1. man	_____		11. woman	_____
2. child	_____		12. mouse	_____
3. deer	_____		13. boy	_____
4. goose	_____		14. pen	_____
5. mouse	_____		15. kite	_____
6. spoon	_____		16. woman	_____
7. child	_____		17. child	_____
8. woman	_____		18. moose	_____
9. sheep	_____		19. man	_____
10. man	_____		20. deer	_____

BE CAREFUL: man . . . men
                                      woman . . . women
                                      child . . . children

Do not add an -s to words that form plurals through the internal change of a letter.

PART C: Signal Words: Singular

A signal word tells you whether a singular or plural usually follows.

This section will deal only with *signal words* that tell you that a *singular* usually follows.

SIGNAL WORDS

one

a

an

each } SINGULAR NOUNS

every

a single

Practice

Write a singular noun after each of these **signal words.**

1. one _____

2. one _____

3. an _____

4. each _____

5. a _____

6. every _____

7. one _____

8. a single _____

9. an _____

10. every _____

11. one _____

12. every _____

13. a _____

14. each _____

15. every _____

16. an _____

17. a single _____

18. an _____

19. one _____

20. each _____

PART D: Signal Words: Plural

These signal words tell you that a *plural* usually follows:

SIGNAL WORDS

two (or more)

both

several

all } PLURAL NOUNS

many

few

some

most

Practice 1

Write a plural noun after each of these **signal words.**

1. many _____
2. six _____
3. most _____
4. several _____
5. some _____
6. four _____
7. all _____
8. both _____
9. all _____
10. few _____

11. both _____
12. several _____
13. nine _____
14. many _____
15. five _____
16. most _____
17. both _____
18. several _____
19. many _____
20. some _____

Practice 2

Write either a singular or a plural noun after these **signal words.** Use as many different nouns as you can think of.

1. a _____
2. some _____
3. few _____
4. a single _____
5. some _____
6. one _____
7. several _____
8. each _____
9. four _____
10. an _____
11. all _____
12. few _____
13. each _____

14. some _____
15. a _____
16. most _____
17. both _____
18. every _____
19. many _____
20. all _____
21. most _____
22. every _____
23. nine _____
24. a _____
25. most _____
26. all _____

27. both _____   34. one _____

28. one _____   35. five _____

29. few _____   36. many _____

30. all _____   37. all _____

31. an _____   38. each _____

32. several _____   39. ten _____

33. a single _____   40. few _____

Practice 3

Write five sentences using signal words that show singular.

1. _____

2. _____

3. _____

4. _____

5. _____

Write five sentences using signal words that show plural.

1. _____

2. _____

3. _____

4. _____

5. _____

PART E: Signal Words with OF

Many signal words are followed by *of* or *of the . . .* Generally, these signal words are followed by a *plural* noun (or a collective noun) because you are really talking about one or more from a larger group.

many of the
some of the   } *students* are . . .
a few of the
lots of the

one of the
each of the   } *students* is . . .

Be careful when you use *one of the* . . . and *each of the* . . . . These groups of signal words are followed by a *plural* noun, but the verb is *singular* because only the signal word (*one* or *each*) is the real subject.*

> *One* of the apples *is* spoiled.
>
> *Each* of the trees *grows* quickly.

Practice   1

Fill in your own nouns in the blanks in these sentences.

1. A lot of _____ are very good.

2. Some of the _____ appear overripe.

3. I bought a few of the _____ on sale last week.

4. He is one of the few _____ who are always absent.

5. That is one of the _____ I can't agree to.

6. We went to the zoo and saw many of the _____ .

7. There are a lot of _____ after the rain.

8. I purchased light bulbs and some of the _____ at the hardware store.

9. Each of the _____ told her story.

10. We raked a lot of _____ in the yard today.

11. I saw one of the _____ at the corner.

12. She heard that some of the _____ were crooked.

13. In the summer, we found lots of _____ .

14. I met a few of the _____ at the dance.

15. Many of the _____ look sick.

16. Each of my _____ has a different personality.

17. I want some of the _____ .

18. That is one of the best _____ I have ever tasted.

19. A few of the _____ cannot read.

20. It was one of the most beautiful _____ we had ever seen.

*See Part G in Chapter 6 for more work on this construction.

Practice 2

Write eight of your own sentences using signal words followed by **of**.

1. _____

_____

2. _____

_____

3. _____

_____

4. _____

_____

5. _____

_____

6. _____

_____

7. _____

_____

8. _____

_____

18

DEMONSTRATIVES (Singular and Plural)

PART A: Defining Demonstratives
PART B: Using THIS and THAT
PART C: Using THESE and THOSE

PART A: Defining Demonstratives

> (1) I want *a* book.
> (2) I want *the* book.
> (3) I want *this* book.
> (4) I want *that* book.

○ Which sentences are *more specific* in terms of which book *I want*?

○ Which sentences almost *demonstrate* which book *I want*?

○ Sentences (3) and (4) *point out* and *demonstrate* which book *I want*.

This and *that* are called *demonstratives* because they point out, demonstrate, and make specific.

PART B: Using THIS and THAT

> (1) I have seen *this* man before.
> (2) I have seen *that* man before.
> (3) Whom does *this* cup of coffee belong to?
> (4) Whom does *that* cup of coffee belong to?

○ Note that in all of these sentences, *this* and *that* precede a *singular* noun.

○ In sentences (3) and (4), which *cup of coffee* is closer to the speaker?

○ In general, *this* is used to point to something close to the speaker.

○ In general, *that* is used to point to something far away from the speaker.

148

Practice   1

Which of these words may be preceded by **this** or **that**? Don't forget: **this** or **that** can be used before *singular* nouns only.

1. _____ book

2. _____ books

3. _____ women

4. _____ airplane

5. _____ English course

6. _____ French courses

7. _____ file cabinets

8. _____ term paper

9. _____ salt shaker

10. _____ friend

Practice   2

Which one of these nouns is close to the speaker and which is far away? Write **C** for **close** or **F** for **far away.**

1. that student _____

2. this boyfriend _____

3. that sweater _____

4. that belt _____

5. this hairdo _____

6. that department _____

7. this paper clip _____

8. this department _____

PART C: Using THESE and THOSE

As you have learned from the preceding sections, *this* and *that* are used before singular nouns.

Should you want to use a demonstrative before a plural noun, use *these and those*.

Singular	Plural
this book . .	these books
that book . .	those books

○ *This* and *these* point to something close to the speaker.

○ *That* and *those* point to something far away from the speaker.

Practice 1

Which one of these words may be preceded by **these** or **those?** Don't forget: **these** or **those** can be used before *plural* nouns only.

1. _____ china plates   6. _____ pencils

2. _____ saucer   7. _____ woman

3. _____ milk container   8. _____ notes

4. _____ milk containers   9. _____ children

5. _____ typewriter   10. _____ paper bags

Practice 2

Write five sentences using **this** or **that,** and five sentences using **these** or **those.**

1. _____

2. _____

3. _____

4. _____

5. _____

6. _____

7. _____

8. _____

9. _____

10. _____

19

ALL ABOUT PRONOUNS

PART A: Defining Pronouns and Antecedents

As you probably know, personal pronouns *take the place of* or *refer to* nouns or other pronouns.

The word that a *pronoun* refers to is called the *antecedent* of the pronoun.

> *Bob* said that (he) was tired.

- *He* refers to *Bob.*
- *Bob* is the antecedent of *he.*

> (He and I) have been good friends ever since (our) college days.

- *Our* refers to *he and I.*
- *He and I* is the antecedent of *our.*

> (Sonia) left early, but I did not see (her) until later.

- *Her* refers to *Sonia.*
- *Sonia* is the antecedent of *her.*

Practice

In each of these sentences, a pronoun has been circled. Write the pronoun and its antecedent in the columns at the right.

	Pronoun	Antecedent
Example: I need the book but can't find (it.)	*it*	*book*
1. Sam and I travel together because (we) are good friends.		
2. Maria is looking for (her) coat.		
3. The students came for (their) grades.		
4. The children waited for me to pick (them) up.		
5. William and Loretta, (you) have to start arriving on time.		
6. My tennis teacher felt that (she) had to raise her fee.		
7. Robert brought those books home because (they) looked interesting.		
8. I saw Tito and gave (him) the money I owed him.		
9. Tito took (his) money and thanked me.		
10. Roberto always gets A's because (he) studies so much.		
11. Where is Dorothy? I can't find (her.)		
12. She and I have been dating for five years; it's time for (us) to settle down.		
13. Harvey, have you done (your) homework?		
14. We drove (our) car all the way to Miami Beach.		

PART B: Pronouns as Subjects

Pronouns have different forms depending on how they function in a sentence.

Pronouns as Subjects

	Singular	Plural
1st person	I	we
2nd person	you	you
3rd person	he, she, it	they

Practice 1

Use the pronoun in each box as the subject of a sentence.

Example: | we | *We are attending college this fall.*

1. | he | _____

2. | it | _____

3. | we | _____

4. | she | _____

5. | they | _____

6. | you | _____

Practice 2

The possible **antecedent** in these sentences appears in parentheses. Choose the pronoun that would most logically take the place of or refer to the antecedent.

Example: (Martha) *She* reads two books a week.

1. (James) _____ left for school early.

2. (James and John) _____ left for school early.

3. After Sally came home from the dance, (Sally) _____ went right to bed.

4. My typewriter is so old that (the typewriter) _____ is not worth repairing.

5. (The students)_____ left the final after the first hour.

6. (The students and I) _____ left the final after the first hour.

7. (Bob) _____ has to leave soon.

8. My teacher said that (my teacher) _____ wants these papers on time.

9. Although the book is long, (the book) _____ reads quickly.

10. Dick bought light green candles. (The candles) _____ look nice on the table.

11. Neil flew to California because (Neil) _____ has relatives there.

12. I saw Mildred as (Mildred) _____ was leaving school.

13. I took calculus this semester, and (the course) _____ was difficult.

14. When a dog is hungry, (a dog) _____ will eat anything.

15. My cousin just started graduate school because (my cousin) _____ wants to get an M.A. in psychology.

PART C: Pronouns as Objects

Pronouns can be objects of either verbs or prepositions.

PRONOUNS AS OBJECTS OF VERBS

Example: I kissed him.

                              ↓
                           object

- ○ The subject does the action—*I.*
- ○ The verb is the action—*kissed.*
- ○ The object receives the action—*him.*

Bob met her at the corner.

- ○ What is the subject? _____ (fill in)
- ○ What is the verb? _____ (fill in)
- ○ What is the object? _____ (fill in)

PRONOUNS AS OBJECTS OF PREPOSITIONS

Prepositions are words that describe direction or place or time—*to, for, near, by, in, on, at, around, between, upon, through,* etc.

Example: The children played around him.

                                    ↓
                                 object

Example: I gave (her) the term papers.

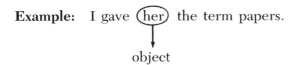

object

$$\left[\begin{array}{l} \text{the preposition } to \\ \text{is often understood} \end{array}\right]$$

Pronouns as Subjects	Pronouns as Objects
I ⟶	me
you ⟶	you (no change)
he ⟶	him
she ⟶	her
it ⟶	it (no change)
we ⟶	us
they ⟶	them

Practice 1

In the parentheses after each pronoun in these sentences, write **S** if the pronoun is a subject or **O** if the pronoun is an object of either a verb or a preposition.

Example: I (*S*) congratulated him (*O*).

1. He ( ) took me ( ) to see the circus. It ( ) was fun.

2. Robert gave her ( ) an engagement ring, and she ( ) appeared happy to receive it ( ).

3. They ( ) saw us ( ) in the classroom. We ( ) were reading books and enjoying them.

4. I ( ) bought them on sale, and they ( ) are the best peaches I ever tasted. I ( ) love them ( ).

5. He ( ) told me ( ) that he ( ) had missed the class and would not really be able to help us ( ).

6. She ( ) gave them ( ) to you ( ) last week.

7. Bob and she ( ) have to meet her ( ) later.

8. We ( ) are going to see a movie today.

9. She ( ) really told him ( ) off after he was two hours late for their date.

10. You ( ) are my ideal of what a student should be. I can't help giving you ( ) A's on all your themes.

Pronouns used as objects also have antecedents.

Example: I know Bob was there because I saw (him.)

antecedent   pronoun

Example: The students did well and the instructor gave (them) A's.

antecedent   pronoun

Practice 2

A pronoun used as an object is circled in each sentence. Write the pronoun and antecedent of the pronoun in the columns on the right.

		Pronoun	**Antecedent**
Example: Those classes were <u>exciting</u> and I am glad that I took (them.)		*them*	*classes*
1. Harvey thought, "What's the matter with (me?")		_____	_____
2. The ties aren't here because I gave (them) away to the Salvation Army.		_____	_____
3. Olga went to the rock concert, where a strange man with red hair spoke to (her.)		_____	_____
4. The instructor said to (him,) "Bob, you are a fine student."		_____	_____
5. The addict realized that life had passed (him) by.		_____	_____
6. Next to (her) was a large dog, but Hortense paid no attention to it.		_____	_____
7. They told (us) that we were wrong although Bernie and I insisted that we were right.		_____	_____
8. Billie, I gave (you) money last week.		_____	_____
9. I used that pen but I can't find (it.)		_____	_____
10. She's always been friendly toward (him,) but Juan is a difficult person to get along with.		_____	_____

PART D: Pronouns that Show Possession

> Bill took his coat and left.

o Whom does *his* refer to? _____ (fill in)

o Who owns the coat? _____ (fill in)

o What is the antecedent of *his*? _____ (fill in)

> We saw our films later that day.

o Whom does *our* refer to? _____ (fill in)

o Who owns the films? _____ (fill in)

o What is the antecedent of *our*? _____ (fill in)

> **Pronouns that Show Possession**
>
> I own *my* . . .
> you own *your* . . .
> he owns *his* . . .
> she owns *her* . . .   } possessions
> it owns *its* . . .
> we own *our* . . .
> they own *their* . .

Practice

In the columns at the right, fill in the pronoun that shows possession or ownership and its antecedent.

	Pronoun of Possession	Antecedent
Example: She took her books.	*her*	*she*
1. Marion saw her friends in the park.	_____	_____
2. Luz, your paper is fantastic.	_____	_____
3. I can't find my paycheck.	_____	_____
4. Robert left his carrots on the table.	_____	_____
5. John and I are taking our vacation together.	_____	_____

6. Pat and Robert are taking their vacation
    together.   _____ _____

7. Bob watched the cat eat its dinner.   _____ _____

8. Bob watched his cat eat.   _____ _____

9. Sylvia is not showing her feelings.   _____ _____

10. The students read their stories in less
    than an hour.   _____ _____

PART E: Review of Pronouns

Reference Chart of Pronouns						
Singular Pronouns				**Plural Pronouns**		
	Subjective	*Objective*	*Possessive*	*Subjective*	*Objective*	*Possessive*
1st:	I	me	my	we	us	our
2nd:	you	you	your	you	you	your
3rd:	he	him	his	they	them	their
	she	her	her			
	it	it	its			

These three forms of pronouns are usually called *cases.*

A pronoun in *subjective case* is the subject of a sentence.

A pronoun in *objective case* is the object of a verb or preposition.

A pronoun in *possessive case* shows possession or ownership.

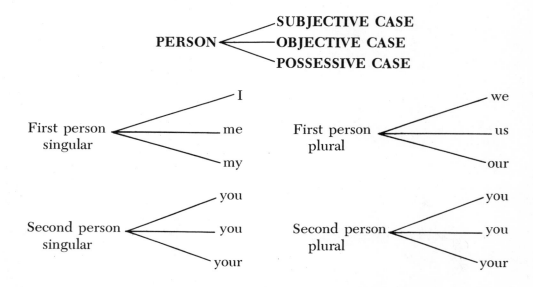

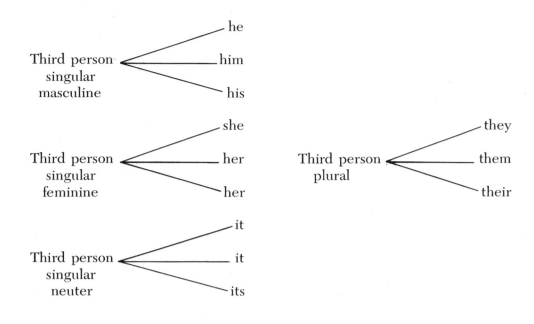

Practice 1

Fill in the correct pronoun.

Example: *she* (sub)
her (poss)
her (obj)

I _____ (sub)	her _____ (poss)	our _____ (poss)
_____ (obj)	_____ (sub)	_____ (sub)
_____ (poss)	_____ (obj)	_____ (obj)
them _____ (obj)	his _____ (poss)	you _____ (obj)
_____ (sub)	_____ (obj)	_____ (sub)
_____ (poss)	_____ (sub)	_____ (poss)
me _____ (obj)	their _____ (poss)	she _____ (sub)
_____ (poss)	_____ (obj)	_____ (poss)
_____ (sub)	_____ (sub)	_____ (obj)
your _____ (poss)	him _____ (obj)	our _____ (poss)
_____ (obj)	_____ (sub)	_____ (obj)
_____ (sub)	_____ (poss)	_____ (sub)

Practice   2

In these sentences, the antecedent is in parentheses. Change the antecedent into the correct pronoun.

Example: (Bill and Sheila) *They* are going to the dance together. It is fun to watch (Bill and Sheila) *them* dance.

1. (Bob) _____ is a good friend of mine. (Bob's) _____ sister and I go to the same college, and (Bob's sister and I) ___ often meet on campus.

2. (Miriam) ___ rarely goes to rock concerts because (rock concerts) ___ are too crowded and noisy for (Miriam) ___ .

3. (The typewriter) ___ is an old model and (the typewriter's) ___ keys are just about worn out.

4. (The typewriters) ___ are old models and (the typewriters') ___ keys are just about worn out.

5. (My final) ___ seemed so easy that I finished (the final) ___ in less than an hour.

6. (Our teachers) ___ gave (my cousin and me) ___ an award.

7. I saw (my parents) ___ on the corner while (my parents) ___ were waiting for (my aunt) ___ to arrive, but (my aunt) ___ never showed up.

8. (Rita) ___ feels that (Rita's) ___ children are better behaved now that (her children) ___ are older and have learned to have respect for (Rita's) ___ problems.

9. (The babies) ___ played with (the babies') ___ toys and everyone watched (the babies) ___ .

10. (The chair) ___ is very nice, but (Billie and Allen's) ___ furniture is usually more modern.

Practice   3

Fill in the correct pronoun (in the boxes) in these sentences. Write the antecedent of the pronoun in the space at the right.

                                                                    Antecedent

Example: Robert decided to go buy some books for his sister's birthday. He bought | *them* | in the Fifth Avenue Book Store.   *books*

1. My keys have been missing for days, and I can't find
    | _____ | anywhere.   _____

2. She was required to purchase [   ] books
    by the end of the second week of classes.   _____

3. Students are required to purchase [   ] books
    by the end of the second week of school.   _____

4. My instructor gave me an A and said [   ] was
    glad to do it.   _____

5. Those tests are much too easy for our students, and I
    think that [   ] shall be changed.   _____

6. Robert and I went to the movies, but [   ]
    couldn't get in. When we tried to sneak in, the usher   _____
    threw [   ] out.   _____

7. This test is much too hard for me and I think that [   ]   _____
    should be changed.

8. You knew you had to do [   ] homework before   _____
    you left for the movies.

9. She is the best student in the class and [   ]   _____
    themes are always a pleasure to read. Moreover, I like
    [   ] as a person.   _____

10. Bowling is a great sport. [   ] is fun, cheap,   _____
    and easy to learn.

11. Bill and Hank always do [   ] homework together,   _____
    and [   ] always do well on finals.   _____

12. Because Frank and I left [   ] change on the   _____
    table, the cashier called out to [   ], "Hey,   _____
    don't you want your money?"

13. The present was too large for the box but we managed
    to close [   ] anyway.   _____

14. "My friends, [   ] are welcome to my home,   _____
    make yourselves comfortable."

PART F: A Problem of Case
(pronouns as subjects)

Don't use the *objective* case when you really want the *subjective* one.
Would *you* write these sentences?

> Me go to the movies.
> Him is my brother.
> Them dance very well.

Aside from the fact that they sound and look strange, what is wrong with
them? Use your Reference Chart of Pronouns and your knowledge of *case* to
explain your answer.

You're right! The pronouns in these sentences are in the objective
case—they *cannot be used* as subjects.

But sometimes students forget about case when they write a subject
composed of two pronouns or a noun and a pronoun.

Bob and (me) have to leave soon.

should be *I*.

Roberta and (him) will be married on Sunday.

should be *he*.

Sam and (her) travel a great deal.

should be _____. (fill in)

Practice   1

Circle the correct pronoun from the choices in parentheses.

Example: Philip and (me, (I)) went for a walk.
(because *I* is in the subjective case)

1. (Him, He) and (I, me) go to the movies once a week.
2. By 4:00, Sheila and (he, him) had already decided to get married.
3. Although John and (her, she) went to the same school, they never met.
4. Sam and (me, I) practice trumpet on Sunday.
5. (Them, They) received gifts for their birthday.
6. Joseph and (he, him) repaired the stereo in two hours.
7. Juan and (her, she) were born in Havana.
8. Deborah and (me, I) met at the dance concert.

In all of these sentences you should have circled the pronoun in the
subjective case.

But be careful! If the pronoun is the *object* of a verb or a preposition, it must be in the *objective* case.

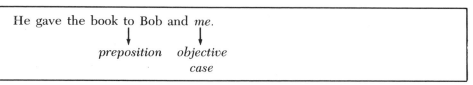

○ If you are not sure, leave out "Bob and." The sentence then reads, "He gave the book to *me.*"

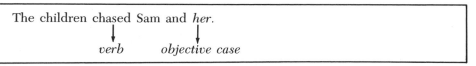

○ Leave out "Sam and." The sentence reads, "The children chased *her.*"

Practice 2

Circle the correct pronoun in the parentheses. If the pronoun is a **subject,** use the **subjective case;** if it is the **object** of a verb or a preposition, use the **objective case.**

1. (We, Us) students want to thank you for a good course.

2. Your class was a treat for (we, us) students.

3. Carlos and (me, I) plan to take Spanish this spring because Mr. Rodriguez will be our teacher.

4. Prof. Simmons gave Lucy and (I, me) the highest grades in the class.

5. Why don't you give (us, we) short people a chance to play basketball?

6. For (we, us), there is nothing like a cold beer on a hot day.

7. The school awarded the coach and (me, I) a medal.

8. We ran after David and (she, her) to give them the money they had left behind.

9. After all, (we, us) people have rights too.

10. The tutor helped my brother and (me, I) with our math homework.

11. Sally and (him, he) played tennis against Tom and (me, I).

12. Jose and (her, she) missed the train.

13. Between you and (me, I), I don't like spinach.

14. Those green apples made Ellen and (him, he) sick.

15. (He, Him) and his wife live alone now that the children are grown.

PART G: A Problem of Case (comparison)*

Comparisons usually follow *than* or *as*:

> (1) He is taller *than* I.

> (2) This helps you as much *as* me.

- In sentence (1), the comparison is completed with a pronoun in the subjective case, *I*.
- In sentence (2), the comparison is completed with a pronoun in the objective case, *me*.

> (1) He is taller than I . . . (am tall).

> (2) This helps you as much as . . . (it helps) . . . me.

- As you can see, a comparison is really a shorthand sentence that purposefully omits words.
- Would you say *me am tall* or *it helps I*?

By completing the comparison (in your head), you can choose the correct case for the pronoun.

Practice   1

Circle the correct pronoun in these comparisons.

1. Water frightens him more than (she, her).

2. My brother is more serious than (she, her).

3. We eat ice cream more often than (they, them).

4. I am as old as (they, them).

5. He is not so old as (we, us).

6. Although our term papers were the same length, the professor gave him a higher grade than (I, me).

7. If you don't think that her friends are as nice as (she, her), why not tell her so?

8. They think they are sharper than (she, her), but wait until they tangle with her and find out the truth.

9. You paid more than (we, us) for that stereo.

10. Sometimes, our children act more mature than (we, us).

11. It often seems to be harder for me than (he, him).

12. Do you think that his sister will be as overweight as (he, him)?

*For work involving comparatives, see Part C in Chapter 20.

Practice 2

Write six sentences using comparisons that are completed with pronouns. Be careful of case!

1. _____

2. _____

3. _____

4. _____

5. _____

6. _____

PART H: Indefinite Pronouns

each
everybody
everyone
nobody
no one
somebody
someone   } All of these words are *singular*.
anybody
anyone
an individual
one
a person

Everyone should do what *he* can to get an A.

Everyone should do . . . ⟨*he*⟩ can . . .

singular   singular
antecedent   pronoun

Each student knew that *he* had done well.

Each student . . . ⟨*he*⟩ had . . .

singular   singular
antecedent   pronoun

If *someone* smiles at you, give *him* a smile in return.

If *someone* smiles . . . give ⟨*him*⟩ . . .

singular   singular
antecedent   pronoun

> *No one* brought *his* book today.

No one . . . (his) book . . .

singular   singular
antecedent   pronoun

Of course, if the *everyone* **or** *individual* **is a woman, use** *she* **or** *her* **rather than** *he* **or** *him.* **Formal English, however, calls for** *he* **or** *him* **when those referred to are both women and men. But many writers now use** *he or she* **in order to cover both the men and the women being referred to.**

Practice 1

Fill in the correct pronouns in the blanks in the sentences below. Then, in the column on the right, write the antecedent of the pronoun that you wrote in the blank.

		Antecedent
Example: Everyone should do *his* best.		*everyone*

1. If a person agrees to do something, _____

   should not go back on _____ word.

2. Each student did _____ paper with ease.

3. One can not blame fate on the stars; everyone is the

   master of _____ own life.

4. Sheila brought _____ date to the party.

5. Somebody climbed in the window and left _____
   footprints in the garden.

6. An individual should always fulfill _____ responsi-

   bility by voting whenever _____ can.

7. My friends will arrive at _____ destination within
   an hour.

8. Someone was here and left _____ mark.

9. People took _____ transistor radios to the beach.

10. Everyone must take _____ seat at exactly 9:30 a.m.

11. I am going to visit _____ parents.

12. You must do _____ homework!   _____

13. A person should take care of _____ health with
    good food and lots of exercise.   _____

14. A person often has to do what _____ doesn't want
    to.   _____

15. Everybody is welcome to try _____ hand at
    figuring out the puzzle.   _____

Practice 2

Now write eight sentences using the indefinite pronouns as antecedents.

1. _____

2. _____

3. _____

4. _____

5. _____

6. _____

7. _____

8. _____

PART I: Collective Nouns

Collective nouns are words that imply more than one person but that are considered singular. Here is a partial list.

group	family
committee	tribe
team	society
class	school
jury	panel
company	college
government	flock

> The *jury* meets early today because *it* must decide on a verdict.

○ *Jury* is the *antecedent* of *it.*

> *Society* must protect *its* members from violence.

    ○ *Society* is the *antecedent* of *its*.

Use *it* or *its* when referring to collective nouns.

Use *they* or *their* only when referring to collective nouns in the plural (schools, companies, etc).

Practice

Fill in the correct pronoun in the blanks in these sentences. Write the antecedent in the box at the right of the sentences.

Antecedent

Example: The committee sent *its* minutes to the president

         of the college.

                                                                      committee

1. The company fired _____ lazy employees.

2. My class is famous for _____ sense of humor.

3. The classes took _____ finals with ease.

4. The Harvard Rowing Team was at _____ best.

5. Most oil companies have raised _____ prices.

6. At 8:00, my college is having _____ annual senior ball.

7. That tribe holds _____ initiation rites every spring.

8. The branches of government have _____ own duties and powers.

9. A great flock of birds sent _____ lonely cry across the lake.

10. The herd moves southward as _____ grazes.

PART J: Special Singular Constructions

either of . . .
neither of . . .
every one of . . . } These antecedents always take *singular* pronouns
each of . . .
one of . . .

Each of the girls did *her* work.

Each ... (*her*) ...

singular singular
antecedent pronoun

Neither of the men finished *his* meal.

Neither ... (*his*) ...

singular singular
antecedent pronoun

Each of the students found out that *he* had passed the test.

Each ... (*he*) ...

singular singular
antecedent pronoun

Practice 1

Fill in the correct pronoun in the space provided in each sentence. Write the antecedent in the box on the right.

Antecedent

Example: Each of the boys did *his* homework. | *each* |

1. One of the children lost _____ hat.

2. The children lost _____ hats.

3. Either of them should be able to do _____ own work.

4. Each of the cats ate _____ dinner.

5. Every one of the women scored high on _____

   verbal test; every one of the men scored high on _____ mathematics test.

6. Neither of the committees has done _____ job well.

7. Each of the women knew that _____ won a scholarship.

8. Both boys brought _____ radios to class.

9. Three Siamese cats sat quietly and ate _____ dinners.

⬜

10. Each of the boys felt that _____ was going to win the chess tournament.

⬜

11. All the boys felt that _____ would win the chess tournament.

⬜

12. One of the books had a scar on _____ binding.

⬜

Practice 2

Now write five sentences using the special singular constructions as antecedents.

1. _____

2. _____

3. _____

4. _____

5. _____

PART K: Pronouns with -self and -selves

Pronouns with *-self* and *-selves* are used in two ways.

(1) Jose washed himself.

(2) The teacher herself thought the test was too difficult.

○ In sentence (1), Jose did something to *himself;* he washed himself (*reflexive*).

○ In sentence (2), *herself* emphasizes the fact that the teacher—much to our surprise—found the test too hard (*intensive*).

	Antecedent	Reflexive and Intensive Pronoun
Singular	I ⟶	myself
	you (singular) ⟶	yourself
	he ⟶	himself
	she ⟶	herself
	it ⟶	itself
Plural	we ⟶	ourselves
	you (plural) ⟶	yourselves
	they ⟶	themselves

Note that in the plural, *-self* is changed to *-selves.*

Practice 1

Fill in the correct intensive or reflexive in the blank space in these sentences. Be careful to match the pronoun with the antecedent.

1. I did it _____ .

2. He _____ was surprised.

3. They bought _____ a present for their anniversary.

4. The cat washed _____ .

5. We had _____ a great time.

6. The student considered _____ the best mathematician in the class.

7. You _____ didn't agree with him.

8. Robert _____ thought the test was easy.

9. Sonia found _____ in a beautiful but strange environment.

10. He wanted the tickets for _____ .

11. We hope to go there _____ .

12. Don't bother, they will get it _____ .

Practice 2

Write five sentences using the reflexive and/or intensive pronouns.

1. _____

2. _____

3. _____

4. _____

5. _____

20

ADJECTIVES AND ADVERBS

PART A: Defining and Writing Adjectives and Adverbs

> (1) Jenny is beautiful.

> (2) Jenny writes beautifully.

- What word in sentence (1) does *beautiful* refer to or describe?

- What word in sentence (2) does *beautifully* refer to or describe?

- *Beautiful* describes Jenny, a noun. *Beautifully*, however, describes not Jenny but how she writes; so *beautifully* describes the verb *writes*, not the noun *Jenny*.

Descriptive words in English have two forms—depending on how they are used. Words like *beautiful* that describe nouns are called *adjectives*.

Words like *beautifully* that describe verbs or adjectives are called *adverbs*. Adverbs usually end in *-ly*.

Practice　1

Write in an appropriate **adjective** from the list at the right to complete each sentence.

1. His face is _____.

2. We live in a/an _____ apartment.

3. _____ remarks are his specialty.

4. John carries a/an _____ case.

5. She wears such _____ clothing.

crowded
purple
sarcastic
ugly
tired
leather
attractive

    The words you wrote in above are adjectives.

    An adjective describes a noun by telling *what kind*.

Practice　2

Write in an appropriate **adverb** from the list at the right to complete each sentence.

1. I write _____ .

2. John gazed at her _____ .

3. The lawyer spoke _____ to the jury.

4. Drive _____ !

5. We always listen _____ to one another.

eloquently
shyly
forcefully
carefully
slowly
pleasantly
admiringly

ly – adverb.

    The words you wrote in are adverbs.

    An adverb describes a verb by telling *how* an action takes place.

    An adverb can also modify an adjective:

Example: He is extremely smart.

      The day feels pleasantly cool.

Most adjectives can be changed into adverbs by adding *-ly:*

    He gave her a *hopeful* glance. (*What kind* of glance?)

    He gazed at her *hopefully*. (*How* did he gaze?)

Practice 3

Change each adjective from the left-hand column into its adverb form in the right-hand column.

Adjective	**Adverb**
1. She is pleasant.	1. She speaks _____
2. She is awkward.	2. She speaks _____
3. We are cautious.	3. We act _____
4. I am decisive.	4. I write _____
5. He is bad.	5. He cooks _____
6. They are graceful.	6. They dance _____
7. I am brilliant.	7. I paint _____
8. He was open.	8. He talked _____
9. It is warm.	9. It shines _____
10. You seemed intense.	10. You gestured _____
11. He is patient.	11. He waits _____
12. She is confident.	12. She sings _____
13. We are distracted.	13. We watched _____
14. We are enthusiastic.	14. We swim _____
15. You are happy.	15. You traveled _____

Practice 4

Circle the adjective or adverb form of the word in parentheses, whichever correctly completes each sentence.

Examples: That is a (bad, badly) example.
                You drive (bad, badly).

1. Terry is a (childish, childishly) person.

2. He behaves (childish, childishly).

3. Writing term papers is easy if you arrange your index cards (systematic, systematically).

4. His story was (convincing, convincingly) told.

5. Wanda paints murals (beautiful, beautifully).   *wall painting - murals*

6. On a very (quiet, quietly) evening, you can hear the waterfall.

7. It was a (seductive, seductively) offer.

8. Hank wrote too (slow, slowly) on the exam.

9. He always writes (slow, slowly).

10. Please speak (clear, clearly).

11. I find this novel very (interesting, interestingly).

12. An (enthusiastic, enthusiastically) lecturer, he keeps our interest.

13. Ethel dresses (attractive, attractively) every day.

14. Talk (soft, softly) or don't talk at all.

15. Leaping (happy, happily) out of bed, the (eager, eagerly) children began their holiday.

16. Sonia was (glad, gladly) that her (painful, painfully) illness was over.

17. You are (surprising, surprisingly) (quiet, quietly) today.

18. She speaks (confident, confidently) and (earnest, earnestly) about the plight of the poor.

19. We are (high, highly) qualified for these jobs.

20. Jerry did not pass the course as (easy, easily) as he thought he would.

Practice 5

Use each adjective and adverb below in a sentence of your own.

Example: careless   *He is a careless person.*

carelessly *He writes carelessly.*

1. illegal _____

illegally _____

2. bad _____

badly _____

3. sweet _____

sweetly _____

4. frequent _____

frequently _____

5. anonymous _____

anonymously _____

PART B: A Troublesome Pair: Good/Well

Unlike most adjectives, *good* does not add *-ly* to become an adverb; it changes to *well*.

Adjective:

> (1) Peter is a *good* student.

Adverb:

> (2) He does *well* in school.

Note, however, that *well* can be used as an adjective to mean *in good health*. For example, *He felt well after his long vacation.*

Practice

Write either **good** or **well** in each sentence below.

Example: Charles plays ball very *well*.

1. My aunt is a _____ cook.

2. She makes _____ Chinese meals.

3. How _____ do you understand the lesson?

4. André knows the material very _____ .

5. It is a _____ thing we have another week to study.

6. He always treats us _____ .

7. How _____ or how badly did Sharon perform?

8. Was her performance _____ or bad?

9. She has a _____ face for modeling.

10. Cynthia doesn't seem _____ ; she doesn't take _____ care of herself.

11. I think mustard goes _____ with all foods, including ice cream.

12. Cynthia thought that particular combination was not very _____ .

PART C: Writing Comparatives with -ER and MORE*

> (1) John is tall.

> (2) John is taller than Mike.

---

*For work involving comparatives followed by pronouns, see Part G in Chapter 19.

○ Sentence (1) simply describes John with the adjective *tall*, but (2) *compares John and Mike* in terms of how tall they are: John is the *taller* of the two.

Taller is called the *comparative* of *tall*.

Use the comparative when you wish to compare two persons or things.

TO FORM COMPARATIVES:

Add *-er* to adjectives and adverbs of *one syllable*.

short	shorter
fast	faster
old	older

Place the word *more* before adjectives and adverbs of *two or more syllables*.

foolish	more foolish
rotten	more rotten
happily	more happily

Practice 1

Write the comparative form of each word below. Either add **-er** to the word or write **more** before it. Never add both **-er** and **more**!

Examples: _____ dumb*er*_____

   __*more*__ willing _____

1. _____ interesting _____

2. _____ hopeful _____

3. _____ thin _____

4. _____ rapidly _____

5. _____ foolish _____

6. _____ clean _____

7. _____ fat _____

8. _____ attractive _____

9. _____ cold _____

10. _____ short _____

11. _____ shameful _____

12. _____ exciting _____

13. _____ light _____

14. _____ young _____

15. _____ solid _____

Here is one important exception to the rule that two-syllable words take *more* to form the comparative:

To show the comparative of two-syllable adjectives ending in -*y*, change the *y* to *i* and add -*er*.

happy	happier
silly	sillier
funny	funnier

Practice 2

Write the comparative form of each adjective below.

Example: happy *happier*

1. sunny _____

2. merry _____

3. friendly _____

4. lazy _____

5. dizzy _____

6. heavy _____

7. dreamy _____

8. creamy _____

9. skinny _____

10. crazy _____

Practice 3

Write a sentence of your own using **the comparative form** of the adjective or adverb listed.

Example: (funny) *This play is funnier than the one we saw last night.*

1. (loud) _____

2. (misty) _____

3. (skillfully) _____

4. (young) _____

5. (lazy) _____

6. (hot) _____

7. (intense) _____

8. (dismal) _____

9. (hopefully) _____

10. (fast) _____

PART D: Writing Superlatives with -EST and MOST

> (1) Tim is the tallest player on the team.

> (2) Juan was voted most useful player.

- In (1), Tim is not just *tall* or *taller than* someone else; he is the *tallest* of all the players on the team.
- In (2), Juan was voted the *most useful of all* the players.

Tallest **and** *most useful* **are called** *superlatives.*

We use the superlative when we wish to compare more than two persons or things.

TO FORM SUPERLATIVES:

Add *-est* to adjectives and adverbs of *one syllable.*

       short   shorter   **shortest**

Place the word *most* before adjectives and adverbs of *two or more syllables.*

       foolish   more foolish   **most foolish**

Exception: With two-syllable adjectives ending in *-y,* change *-y* to *-i* and add *-est.*

       happy   happier   **happiest**

Practice   1

Write the superlative form of each word below. Add either -est or most, not both.

Examples: _____ tall*est* _____

      ____*most*___ ridiculous _____

1. _____ dark _____

2. _____ colorful _____

3. _____ heavy _____

4. _____ thick _____

5. _____ brilliant _____

6. _____ courageously _____

7. _____ remarkable _____

8. _____ frightening _____

9. _____ blue _____

10. _____ clear _____

Practice 2

Make the *italicized* words below into superlatives and use each phrase in a sentence of your own.

Example: (dumb dog) <u>*This is the dumbest dog I've ever seen.*</u>

1. (*intelligent* person) _____

   _____

2. (*dull* book) _____

   _____

3. (*cloudy* sky) _____

   _____

4. (*colorful* sweater) _____

   _____

5. (*tiny* baby) _____

   _____

6. (*fast* train) _____

   _____

PART E: Troublesome Comparatives and Superlatives

These four words are some of the trickiest you will learn:

	Comparative	Superlative
Adjective: good	better	best
Adverb: well	better	best
Adjective: bad	worse	worst
Adverb: badly	worse	worst - the most

Practice

Fill in the correct comparative or superlative form of the word in parentheses. Remember, **better** and **worse** compare **two** persons or things. **Best** and **worst** are superlatives, super good or super bad.

Example: Is this theme *better* than my last one? (good)
(Here, two themes are compared.)

Example: It was the *worst* movie I have ever seen. (bad)
(Of *all* movies, it was the *most* awful.)

1. I like cake _better_ than candy. (well)

2. I like chocolate cake the _best_ . (well)

3. The weather has been _better_ this year than last. (good)

4. The team played _worse_ than it did last year. (badly)

5. It is the _worst_ team in the league. (bad)

6. This watch works _better_ than my old one. (well)

7. The situation is _worse_ than ever before. (bad)

8. It could be _worse_ . (bad)

9. I hope my _worst_ fears do not come true. (bad)

10. Of the two, Cheryl is the _better_ pianist. (good)

11. Of all of us, Cheryl is the _best_ pianist. (good)

12. He is one of the _best_ poets in town. (good)

13. He is also one of the _worst_ public speakers. (bad)

14. For _____ (good) or for _____ (bad), we promised to stick together.

15. Is your friend feeling _____ ? (bad)

UNIT V
MECHANICS

21
APOSTROPHE

PART A: **Using the Apostrophe for Contractions**
PART B: **Defining the Possessive**
PART C: **Using the Apostrophe to Show Possession (in words that do not already end in -s)**
PART D: **Using the Apostrophe to Show Possession (in words that already end in -s)**

PART A: Using the Apostrophe for Contractions

A contraction is a way of combining two words and making one word out of them.

Example: do not = don't

Note that the *o* of *not* is omitted in the contraction. An apostrophe (') is placed in the spot where the *o* had been to show that a letter is being omitted.

Examples: should + not = shouldn't ("o" omitted)
I + have = I've ("ha" omitted)

Practice   1

Write these as contractions:

1. I + will = _____ I'll _____
2. you + are = _____ you're _____
3. will + not = _____ won's w _____
4. who + is = _____ who' _____
5. it + has = _____ it's _____

6. they + will = _____ they'll _____
7. he + is = _____ hi's _____
8. you + have = _____ you've _____
9. she + will = _____ she'll _____
10. they + are = _____ they've _____

182

11. she + has = _____she's_____   14. does + not = _____doesn't_____

12. they + will = _____they'll_____   15. I + shall = _____I'll_____

13. would + not = _____wouldn't_____   16. that paper + is = _____paper's_____

NOTE: *Won't* is an odd contraction because it cannot be broken into its components in the same way the contractions above can.

will + not = won't

Practice 2

Supply the missing apostrophes.

1. Hell go to school in the fall.

2. Its raining.

3. Hes not here now.

4. Youre supposed to leave soon.

5. Theyre at home.

6. Whos at the door?

7. Whats that for?

8. Its hard to do homework when the television is on.

9. Shell be in Europe soon.

10. Theyre going to the theater next week.

Practice 3

Write five sentences using the apostrophe in a contraction.

1. _____

2. _____

3. _____

4. _____

5. _____

PART B: Defining the Possessive

A possessive is a way of showing that someone or something owns something or someone else.

Practice

In these phrases, who owns what?

Example: "the hat of the man" **means** *the man owns the hat*

1. "the shoes of Mary" **means** _____

2. "the personality of the teacher" **means** _____

3. "the office of the dean" **means** _____

4. "the toys of the children" **means** _____

5. "the power of the people" **means** _____

6. "the love of women" **means** _____

7. "the notebooks of the students" **means** _____

8. "the husband of the cousin of my friend" **means** _M_____

PART C: Using the Apostrophe to Show Possession (in words that do not already end in -s)

> (1) the book of my father

becomes

> (2) my father's book

○ In phrase (1), who owns what? _____(fill in)
○ In phrase (1), what is the *owner* word? _____(fill in)
○ How does the *owner* word show possession in phrase (2)?

_____ (fill in)

If the *owner* word (possessive) does not end in an -s, add an apostrophe and an -s to show possession.

Practice   1

Change these phrases into possessives with an apostrophe and an **s.**

Example: the friend of my uncle

becomes

my uncle's friend

Note that the **owner** words **do not end in -s.**

1. the text of the instructor = _____

2. a son of that woman = _____

3. the daughter of that man = _____

4. the vacation of a week = _____

5. the needs of the student = _____

Practice 2

Write eight sentences that use an apostrophe to show ownership. Use **owner** words that do not already end in **-s.**

1. _____

2. _____

3. _____

4. _____

5. _____

6. _____

7. _____

8. _____

PART D: Using the Apostrophe to Show Possession (in words that already end in -s)

> (1) the toys of the girls

becomes

> (2) the girls' toys

○ In phrase (1), who owns what? _____ (fill in)

○ In phrase (1), what is the *owner* word? _____ (fill in)

○ How does the *owner* word show possession in phrase (2)?

_____ (fill in)

If the *owner* word (possessive) ends in an -*s*, add an apostrophe after the -s.*

*Many writers add an '*s* to one-syllable proper names that end in -*s*.

Practice 1

Change these phrases into possessives with an apostrophe.

1. the marks of the instructors = _____

2. a residence of the students = _____

3. the car of my cousins = _____

4. the papers of these pupils = _____

5. the present of the aunts = _____

Practice 2

Write eight sentences that use an apostrophe to show ownership. Use **owner** words that ends in **-s.**

1. _____
2. _____
3. _____
4. _____
5. _____
6. _____
7. _____
8. _____

Practice 3

Rewrite each of the following groups of short sentences as **one** sentence by using a possessive.

Example: Joan has a friend. The friend comes from Chile.
             Joan's friend comes from Chile.

1. Tom has a mother. His mother flies jet planes.

   _____

2. The people have a committee. The committee is making changes.

   _____

3. Linda has a child. The child is sick with the flu.

   _____

4. John has a girl friend. She knows astrology.

   _____

5. Mr. Jones owns a cobra. The cobra is very friendly.

   _____

6. A woman has a place. The place is not in the home anymore.

   _____

7. Bobbie has a class. Her class meets in Gould Hall.

   _____

8. My uncles have a friend. The friend has a basement. The basement is loaded with fascinating things.

   _____

BE CAREFUL

Remember that the apostrophe is used to show possession by nouns. No apostrophe is used in possessive pronouns (underlined below):

Singular	Plural
my book	our book
your book	your book
his book	
her book	their book
its book	

Do not confuse *its* (possessive pronoun) with *it's* (contraction for *it is* or *it has*) or *your* (possessive pronoun) with *you're* (contraction for *you are*).*

*See the section on Look Alikes/Sound Alikes for extra work.

22

COMMA

The comma is a pause. It gives your reader a chance to stop for a moment, to think about where your sentence has been and where it is going, and to prepare to read on.

Although this chapter will cover some basic uses of the comma, there is one generalization you should always keep in mind—if there is no reason for a comma, leave it out!

PART A: Commas for Direct Address

> Bob, you must leave now.

> You must, Bob, leave now.

> You must leave now, Bob.

- ○ Bob is the person spoken to; he is being addressed directly.
- ○ His name—the person addressed—is set off by commas whenever it appears in the sentence.

Practice   1

Circle the person or persons being directly addressed and punctuate the sentence correctly.

1. Larry help me carry these heavy packages.

2. I tell you my friends that I could care less.

3. You know Father it's too cold to play football today.

4. Will you be able to help me with my paper tonight Susan?

5. I think Marsha that you ought to go to graduate school.

6. Now I have you in my clutches my proud beauty.

7. Get out of my roast you mangy old dog.

8. As I see it Sid you have only one option—scratch the horse's nose.

9. O.K. folks the show's over.

10. My dear child there is no Santa Claus.

Practice 2

Write five sentences using direct address. Punctuate correctly.

1. _____

2. _____

3. _____

4. _____

5. _____

PART B: Commas for Parenthetical Expressions

> By the way, I think you're beautiful.

> I think, by the way, that you're beautiful.

> I think that you're beautiful, by the way.

○ "By the way" *modifies* or *qualifies* the entire sentence or idea.
○ It is called *parenthetical* because it seems to be almost a side remark, something that could be placed in parentheses: *(by the way) I think that you're beautiful.*
○ Set off a *parenthetical expression* with commas.

Here are some more parenthetical expressions (but not a complete list):

as a matter of fact	in fact
to tell the truth	in the first place
it seems to me	last of all
for example	

Practice 1

Circle the parenthetical expression and then set it off by commas.

1. To begin with I want to see the manager.
2. He is in fact a slob.
3. The customers it seems never stop complaining.
4. She possesses it would seem psychic powers.
5. Honestly it was an accident.
6. This paper I feel isn't adequate.
7. In truth I didn't like the ballet.
8. This is not a good idea by the way.
9. The instructor insists for example that I write three term papers.
10. My latest book I hope will sell a million copies.

Practice 2

Write five sentences using parenthetical expressions. Punctuate correctly.

1. _____
2. _____
3. _____
4. _____
5. _____

PART C: Commas for Addresses

My teacher moved from 300 Foster Place, Brooklyn, New York, to Boston, Massachusetts.

- Note that commas separate different parts of an address.
- Note that a comma follows the last item in an address (Brooklyn, New York, to . . .) .

But . . .

Julio Smith *from* Queens is the new president of the Brooklyn Spanish Club.

- A one-word address preceded by a preposition (*in, on, at, near, from,* etc.) is not followed by a comma unless there is *another* reason for it.

But . . .

> Julio Smith, Queens, is the new president of the Brooklyn Spanish Club.

○ Commas are required in a one-word address if the preposition is omitted.

Practice 1

Punctuate correctly.

1. The class traveled to the Botanical Gardens Park Place Sydney Australia.
2. My buddy from Jamaica is making a special dinner for us at his house 60 Ventnor Ave.
3. The doctor has a beautiful office near St. Marks Place.
4. Who lives at 9999 Ninth Avenue New York New York?
5. I live near Valentine Avenue and close to the park.
6. There is an Amsterdam New York and an Amsterdam Netherlands.
7. Grant's Department Store 20–27 Selwyn Avenue Staten Island New York is having a sale on karate belts.
8. His father lives in San Juan Puerto Rico, but his sister has never been out of Queens.

Practice 2

Write five sentences using addresses. Punctuate correctly.

1. _____
2. _____
3. _____
4. _____
5. _____

PART D: Commas for Dates

> I arrived on Tuesday, March 18, 1972, and found that I was in the wrong city.

○ Note that commas separate the different parts of the date.
○ Note that a comma follows the last item in a date.

But . . .

> She saw him on Wednesday and spoke with him.

○ A one-word date preceded by a preposition is not followed by a comma (unless there is another reason for it).

Practice 1

Punctuate correctly.

1. I was born on January 10 1945 in a small New England town.

2. By Wednesday June 8 1957 I had already graduated from college.

3. Your book is at the Downtown Library, where it has been waiting for you since April 19 1976.

4. On February 5 1900 the Athletic Club voted him into membership.

5. Friday June 18 was my lucky day.

Practice 2

Write five sentences using dates. Punctuate correctly.

1. _____

2. _____

3. _____

4. _____

5. _____

PART E: Commas after Introductory Phrases

> (1) By the end of the season, our team will have won 30 games straight.

○ "By the end of the season" *introduces* the main idea.
○ An *introductory phrase* is usually followed by a comma.

> (2) On Thursday we left for Hawaii.

○ A very short introductory phrase need not be followed by a comma.

Practice 1

Punctuate correctly.

1. At the time of his arrival the rain had already stopped.

2. In the middle of the afternoon the four boys left their trailer in search of water.

3. Every Thursday at 3:00 he walks into the store to purchase a chocolate bar.

4. By noon she had exercised all that she had wanted to.

5. During my stay at this college I have found that the deans are very helpful.

6. After such hot weather I always feel ready for a vacation at the North Pole.

7. Before the end of the party let me tell you how nice it's been.

8. Near the end of the day the player was so tired that she could barely pick up the bat.

Practice 2

Write five sentences using introductory phrases. Punctuate correctly.

1. _____

2. _____

3. _____

4. _____

5. _____

PART F: Commas to Set Off Appositives

> (1) The Rialto, a new theater, is on 10th Street.

○ A *new theater* describes *Rialto*.

> (2) An old man, my grandfather can barely walk.

○ What group of words describes *grandfather*? _____

_____ (fill in)

> (3) They bought a new painting, a rather beautiful landscape.

○ What group of words describes *painting*? _____

_____ (fill in)

○ *A new theater, an old man, a rather beautiful landscape* are called *appositives*.

An appositive is usually a group of words that describes a noun or pronoun. It can occur at the beginning (1), middle (2), or end (3) of a sentence.

An appositive is set off by commas.

Practice 1

Circle the appositive and punctuate correctly.

1. Her instructor an expert on African affairs sponsored a trip to Ghana.

2. A white cat especially a Persian will leave a trail of fur throughout your home.

3. Pickles my favorite food make my lips pucker.

4. She hopes to go to Central Medical School a fine institution.

5. A short man he decided not to pick a fight with the basketball player.

6. That man the one standing on the corner is a known drug-pusher.

7. Robert a prize fighter is not allowed to use his fists in a fight.

8. Jose told Mario his second cousin to pick him up at the corner.

BE CAREFUL:

A one-word appositive is usually not set off by commas.

Examples: My friend Bill is not here.
Fernando's uncle Sam is a computer programmer.

Practice   2

Write five sentences using the appositive. Punctuate correctly.

1. _____

2. _____

3. _____

4. _____

5. _____

PART G: Commas in Items in a Series

(1) I like apples, oranges, and pears.

○ What three things do *I like*? _____ , _____ , and

_____ (fill in)

Use commas to separate three or more items in a series.

(2) We will walk through the park, take in a film, and visit a friend.

○ What three things will *we do*? _____ , _____ , and

_____ (fill in)

(3) She loves to walk through ethnic neighborhoods sample odd foods and
learn foreign languages.

○ What are the items in a series? _____

_____ and _____(fill in).

○ Punctuate sentence (3).

But:

If you want to join three or more items with *and* or *or*, do not use commas.

> (4) She plays tennis *and* golf *and* softball.

○ Note that commas are not used in sentence (4).

Practice   1

Punctuate correctly.

1. I can't find my shoes my socks or my underwear.
2. I studied hard worked long hours and still couldn't pass the test.
3. The top of the refrigerator was cluttered with a watermelon a glass of milk and a tuna sandwich.
4. The postman brings mail in snow in sleet and in rough weather.
5. Francine went to the wrestling match Harry visited the antique show and Isaac caught a bus for L.A.
6. By the end of the party, everyone was well-fed and happy and tired.
7. I am sick of writing term papers reading textbooks and listening to teachers drone on.
8. She plans to be a civil rights lawyer her brother is going into a seminary and her sister just wants to paint beautiful pictures.

Practice   2

Write five sentences containing three or more items in a series. Punctuate correctly.

1. _____

2. _____

3. _____

4. _____

5. _____

23

DIRECT AND INDIRECT QUOTATION

PART A: Defining Direct and Indirect Quotations
PART B: Punctuating Simple Direct Quotations
PART C: Punctuating Split Quotations
PART D: End Punctuating Quotations

PART A: Defining Direct and Indirect Quotations

> (1) John said that he was going.

> (2) John said, "I am going."

- ○ Which sentence gives the *exact words* of the speaker (John)?
- ○ Why is sentence (2) called a *direct quotation?*
- ○ Why is sentence (1) called an *indirect quotation?*
- ○ Note that *that* introduces the *indirect quotation.*

Practice

Write **I** in the space at the right if the sentence uses an **indirect quotation;** write a **D** in the space at the right if the sentence is a **direct quotation.**

1. I answered that I was leaving early.   _____

2. Rita asked, "Where is my pen?"   _____

3. Robert felt it was a good day to be in the park.   _____

4. The students called, "Get out of the building; it's a fire!"   _____

5. "This is silly," she exclaimed.   _____

6. He hoped that I was well.   _____

7. "Don't leave now," they begged.   _____

8. "I now pronounce you man and wife," the preacher said.   _____

PART B: Punctuating Simple Direct Quotations

Rafael whispered, "Yes, I love you."

Note the punctuation:
- A comma before the direct quotation
- Quotation marks around the speaker's exact words
- Capital letter for first word of direct quotation
- A period inside the quotation marks

Of course, the direct quotation may come first in the sentence.

"Yes, I love you," Rafael whispered.

- List the rules for a direct quotation written this way:

_____

_____

_____

_____

Practice 1

Rewrite these simple direct quotations, punctuating them correctly.

1. They murmured let's leave now.

    Rewrite: _____

2. The child cried I want my mommy.

    Rewrite: _____

3. It's raining we mumbled angrily.

    Rewrite: _____

4. Looking at the flowers, Bob said I never saw a yellow rose before.

    Rewrite: _____

5. We are starving the puppies seemed to be barking.

   Rewrite: _____

6. Your shirt is filthy exclaimed his father.

   Rewrite: _____

7. He said to me somehow I don't believe you.

   Rewrite: _____

8. The professor warned them your papers must be in on time.

   Rewrite: _____

Practice 2

Write five sentences with simple direct quotations.

1. _____

2. _____

3. _____

4. _____

5. _____

PART C: Punctuating Split Quotations

Sometimes a direct quotation is split into two parts:

> "Because it is 2 a.m.," he said, "you had better go."

- The *he said* is set off by commas.
- The second part—*you had better go*—begins with a small letter because it is part of the first directly quoted words.

> "Because it is 2 a.m. . . you had better go."

A direct quotation may also be broken into separate sentences:

> "It is a long ride to San Francisco," he said. "We should leave early."

- Since the second part of the quotation is a separate sentence, it begins with a capital letter.

BE CAREFUL!

If you break a direct quotation into separate sentences, be sure that both parts of the quotation are complete sentences.

Practice 1

Rewrite these **split** direct quotations, punctuating them correctly.

1. If you are tired she said you might as well leave now.

   Rewrite: _____

2. Don't drive so fast he begged I get nervous.

   Rewrite: _____

3. Since it is Thursday we replied we have French today.

   Rewrite: _____

4. I want to go to Puerto Rico he told me I have relatives there.

   Rewrite: _____

5. She dislikes me her teacher answered because she thinks that I am prejudiced.

   Rewrite: _____

6. Riding a motocycle she informed us can be a lot of fun.

   Rewrite: _____

7. This catalogue is fantastic the clerk said and you can have it for free.

   Rewrite: _____

8. I have to read this novel by Tuesday he moaned but I don't think I will have time.

   Rewrite: _____

Practice 2

Write five sentences using split quotations.

1. _____

2. _____

3. _____

4. _____

5. _____

PART D: End Punctuating Quotations

A sentence may end in any one of three ways.

- a period (.)
- a question mark (?)
- an exclamation point (!)

The *period* (.) is *always* placed inside the quotation mark.

> He said, "My car costs $3,000."

The question mark (?) and the exclamation point (!) may go before or after the quotation marks—depending on the sense of the sentence.

(1)   (2)

> He asked, "Where are you?"   Did he say, "I am 32 years old"?

- The question mark in sentence (1) is placed before the end quotation marks because the direct quotation is a question.
- The question mark in sentence (2) is placed after the end quotation marks because the direct quotation itself *is not a question.*

Note that sentence (1) can be reversed:

> "Where are you?" he asked.

(3)

> She yelled, "Help!"

- Can you formulate the rules for the exclamation point?

_____

_____

_____

_____

- Note that sentence (3) can be reversed:

> "Help!" she yelled.

Practice

Rewrite these direct quotations, punctuating them correctly.

1. She asked why did you do that.

   Rewrite: _____

2. He screamed I hate parsley.

   Rewrite: _____

3. Did you say the frost is on the pumpkin.

   Rewrite: _____

4. Don't blame me he insisted.

   Rewrite: _____

5. How do you do he asked.

   Rewrite: _____

6. The students cheered we want more English courses.

   Rewrite: _____

7. My uncle thought how can I leave without being seen.

   Rewrite: _____

24
CAPITALIZATION

1. nationality, race, _____ Protestant, Jewish, American,
   language, religion   Negro, Catholic, French, English,
                                      etc.

This group is *always* **capitalized.**

2. states, cities,   Pacific Ocean, New Zealand,
   bodies of water,   Capital . . . Harlem, California, Central Park,
   places, streets, etc.   Jones Street, etc.
                      But . . .
                                  the lake, a town, a large state,
                                  etc.

If you name the specific state, city, street, etc., **capitalize;** if you don't, use
small letters.

                                  Empire State Building, Paradise
                                  Theater, National Organization of
                                  Women, Johnson City Library,
                      Capital . . . Smithson University, etc.
3. buildings, organiza-
   tions, institutions
                      But . . .   a tall building, an expensive
                                  theater, a feminist group,
                                  an old school, etc.

If you name the specific building, etc., **capitalize;** if you don't, use small
letters.

4. historical events, historical periods, documents

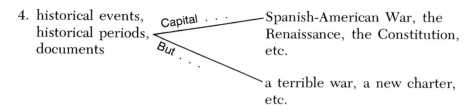

Capital . . . —Spanish-American War, the Renaissance, the Constitution, etc.

But . . . —a terrible war, a new charter, etc.

If you name the specific historical event, document, etc., **capitalize;** if you don't, use small letters.

5. months, days, holidays, seasons

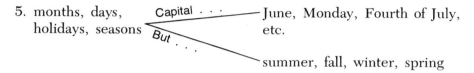

Capital . . . —June, Monday, Fourth of July, etc.

But . . . —summer, fall, winter, spring

Always **capitalize** months, days, and holidays; use small letters for seasons.

6. professional titles

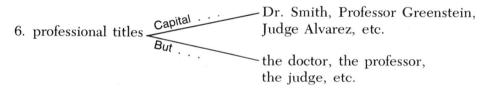

Capital . . . —Dr. Smith, Professor Greenstein, Judge Alvarez, etc.

But . . . —the doctor, the professor, the judge, etc.

If you name the doctor, judge, etc., **capitalize;** if you don't, use small letters.

7. family relationship

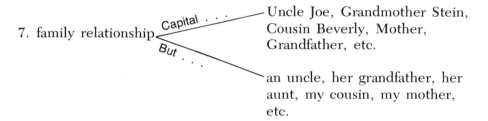

Capital . . . —Uncle Joe, Grandmother Stein, Cousin Beverly, Mother, Grandfather, etc.

But . . . —an uncle, her grandfather, her aunt, my cousin, my mother, etc.

If you name the relative or use *Mother, Father, Grandmother* or *Grandfather* as a name, **capitalize;** however, if these words are preceded by a possessive pronoun, an article or an adjective, use small letters.

8. brand names ——————— Greaso hair oil, Quick drafting ink, etc.

Capitalize the brand name but not the type of product.

9. geographic location

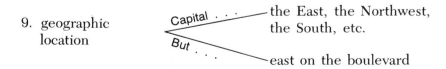

Capital . . . —the East, the Northwest, the South, etc.

But . . . —east on the boulevard

If you mean a geographic location, **capitalize;** if you mean a direction, use small letters.

10. academic   Capital . . . ———Mathematics 51, Sociology 11,
    subjects   World Literature 11
                      But . . .
                                   ———tough mathematics course, an **A**
                                      in sociology, etc.

If you use the course number, **capitalize;** if you don't, use small letters
(except for languages).

11. titles of books, ——————————— <u>A Farewell to Arms,</u>
    poems, plays, films   "Ode to a Bat"

Capitalize titles except for short words or prepositions, but the *first* and *last*
words of the title *must be* capitalized.

Practice

Capitalize where necessary.

1. The yellowstone national park is a fun place to visit.

2. I don't think that this judge is corrupt, but I know that senator south takes bribes.

3. Have you seen my uncle frank today? He is supposed to be visiting my cousin.

4. Have you ever read the declaration of independence?

5. I'm from nigeria, but I have been in the united states for ten years.

6. Although the swimming at lake george is excellent, I want to spend my summer by the sea.

7. Funny, you don't look italian.

8. He just bought ten decca records on friday.

9. Do you plan to take psychology this semester?

10. I went to a good school, thoreau high school.

11. We are taking a trip to the south for the winter.

12. Wait until you take a course with professor miranda!

13. Victor, have you seen mother?

14. No one really discovered the pacific ocean; it was always there.

15. I have just read "the deserted village" and loved it.

16. I love spring but dislike the fall, except for thanksgiving.

17. She plans to go camping this summer in the northwest.

18. If you continue driving east, you will end up in the swamp.

19. Did you get that beanbag for christmas?

20. This photograph of my grandfather is beautiful.

A/AN/AND

1. *A* is used before a word beginning with a consonant or a consonant sound.

Examples: *a* dog, *a* cat, *a* book, *a* pen, *a* uniform.

2. *An* is used before a word beginning with a vowel (*a, e, i, o, u*) or a silent *h*.

Examples: *an* airplane, *an* hour, *an* eagle, *an* orange

Write *an hour* because the *h* in hour is silent, but write *a house* because the *h* in house is not silent.

3. *And* joins words or ideas together.

Examples: John *and* Robert play baseball on Sunday.
I like apples *and* oranges.
He is a good student, *and* he knows it.

Practice 1

1. Carole sings _____ great deal.

2. He reads _____ book _____ day.

3. She can write _____ essay in two hours.

4. John ＿＿ Mike went to ＿＿ baseball game.

5. My cousin lives in ＿＿ igloo.

6. Yesterday, I saw ＿＿ man sitting on ＿＿ elk.

7. The animal disappeared into ＿＿ hole in the ground.

8. ＿＿ ant is ＿＿ very strong insect.

9. My brother ＿＿ I have ＿＿ old car.

10. The bottle has ＿＿ interesting shape ＿＿ it will look nice as ＿＿ vase.

11. ＿＿ what's going on here?

12. It's ＿＿ good day to walk for ＿＿ hour ＿＿ visit ＿＿ friend.

13. He hopes that ＿＿ large car will give ＿＿ smoother ride, but ＿＿ large car gets only 5

    or 6 miles to ＿＿ gallon.

14. She is bright ＿＿ thoughtful, but her brother is ＿＿ poor student ＿＿ ＿＿
    inconsiderate person.

15. The apartment is ＿＿ good buy even though there is ＿＿ crack in the kitchen wall.

Practice   2

Write three sentences using **an,** three using **a,** and three using **and.**

1. _____

2. _____

3. _____

4. _____

5. _____

6. _____

7. _____

8. _____

9. _____

ALREADY/ALL READY

1. *Already* means at this time or before.

Examples: He had *already* left by the time we arrived.
I *already* know how to drive, so I don't need lessons.

2. *All ready* means everything is ready.

Examples: The children are *all ready* to leave for camp.
The dinner is not *all ready* yet.

Practice   1

1. He is _____ the best athlete in school; what more can you ask for?

2. Are you _____ for school?

3. The drinks were _____ for the guests.

4. Has he arrived _____ ?

5. Sorry, the doctor has _____ gone for the day.

6. He has _____ polished his shoes; now he has to comb his hair.

7. Have you _____ gotten your clothing for the trip?

8. I guess you're not _____ yet.

9. He had _____ won the scholarship when his student loan came through.

10. I hope you will be _____ by 4:00 PM.

Practice   2

Write three sentences using **already** and three using **all ready.**

1. _____

2. _____

3. _____

4. _____

5. _____

6. _____

BUY/BY

1. *Buy* means to purchase.

Examples: I want to *buy* a new hat.
He *buys* a new car every year.

2. *By* means next to, near, according to, etc.

Examples: I walked *by* my old apartment house.
By the lake is a large old-fashioned cottage.

Practice   1

1. _____ the time I reached the bus stop, the bus had pulled away.

2. I always remember to _____ milk after the grocery store is closed.

3. I walked _____ the drugstore and remembered that I had to _____ aspirin.

4. I expect to be home _____ ten o'clock.

5. _____ my standards, the composition was very good.

6. They knew the child was sick _____ the harsh sound of his cry.

7. When I get hungry, I run over to the store and _____ candy.

8. New York and Chicago _____ subway cars from Ford Motor Co.

9. The bus route passes right _____ my apartment building.

10. How old do you have to be to _____ alcohol in California?

11. The family will _____ enough groceries for a week.

12. We could tell _____ his smile that he was telling a lie.

Practice   2

Write three sentences using **buy** and three using **by**.

1. _____

2. _____

3. _____

4. _____

5. _____

6. _____

IT'S/ITS

1. *It's* is a contraction of it + is or it + has. If you cannot substitute it is or it has in the sentence, you cannot use it's.

Examples: *It's* raining. = It is raining.
              It's been a hard day = It has been a hard day.

2. *Its* is a possessive; it shows ownership.

Examples: The dog gnawed *its* bone.
              The baby played with *its* rattle.

Practice   1

1. _____ too difficult a problem for me.

2. The chair had a hole in _____ seat.

3. _____ been a long time since I've seen you.

4. _____ not a hard test.

5. The lamp looks _____ best on that table.

6. If _____ too late, let's not go home at all.

7. _____ never been my favorite sport.

8. The government is doing _____ best.

9. I hope _____ not too cold tomorrow.

10. If _____ O.K. with you, I am leaving now.

11. _____ good that you're early.

12. I hope _____ ready on time.

13. I know _____ a spark-plug, but what is _____ purpose?

14. I don't think that _____ a good idea.

Practice   2

Write three sentences using **it's** and three using **its.**

1. _____

2. _____

3. _____

4. _____

5. _____

6. _____

LOSE/LOOSE

1. *Lose* means to misplace, to accidentally leave behind.

Example: Did you *lose* your homework?

2. *Loose* means ill-fitting, too large.

Example: That shirt is *loose* around the collar; it looks terrible.

Practice   1

1. He tightened the _____ screw.

2. I tried not to _____ my wallet.

3. This radio has a _____ connection.

4. People _____ their minds for many different reasons.

5. The _____ clothing of desert travelers is designed for comfort.

6. It's a sad day when the Mets _____ a home game.

7. Everything becomes _____ as a car gets old.

8. If you _____ your way at night, find a cop.

9. He could not _____ the men who were following him.

10. The sweater was of a very _____ knit.

Practice   2

Write three sentences using **lose** and three using **loose**.

1. _____

2. _____

3. _____

4. _____

5. _____

6. _____

PAST/PASSED

1. *Past* is that which has already occurred—it is over with.

Examples: It's hard to forget one's *past*.
                His past is not very pleasant.

2. *Passed* is the past tense of the verb pass.

Examples: He *passed* her in the hallway.
                They *passed* the store on the way home.

Practice   1

1. They are having trouble with the _____ tense.

2. Our friends _____ us and said, "Hello."

3. We _____ the store but didn't go in.

4. The moon _____ in front of the sun.

5. He was living in the _____ .

6. All her problems are caused by _____ mistakes.

7. My grandmother was 90 when she _____ away.

8. The bullet _____ by his ear.

9. Don't let your _____ interfere with your hopes for the future.

10. In the _____ , he always _____ here at ten o'clock.

11. Joan's boyfriend _____ while she was in the shop.

12. They _____ him a sandwich.

Practice   2

Write three sentences using **past** and three using **passed.**

1. _____

2. _____

3. _____

4. _____

5. _____

6. _____

RISE/RAISE

1. *Rise* **means to get up by one's own power.**

    ○ The past tense of *rise* is *rose.*

    ○ The past participle of *rise* is *risen.*

Examples: The sun *rises* at 6 a.m.
            The balloon *rose* towards the clouds.
            He *had risen* from his seat.

2. *Raise* **means to lift an object.**

    ○ The past tense of *raise* is *raised.*

    ○ The past participle of *raise* is *raised.*

Examples: *Raise* your left hand.
            She *raised* the weights.
            The truck *had raised* the ton of sand.

Practice   1

1. Can you _____ that piano another inch or two?

2. Hot air _____ .

3. Look at the sky; the moon has _____ .

4. The student _____ his hand in order to answer the question.

5. They _____ from their seats and left the room.

6. The corporal _____ the flag every day.

7. The oil _____ to the top of the solution.

8. What time do you usually _____ in the morning?

9. That picture should be _____ another foot.

10. He _____ the vase and dusted underneath it.

11. The balloon _____ and flew off towards the ocean.

12. We _____ the canoe to our shoulders.

13. He had already _____ from his seat by the time the teacher said, "Sit down!"

14. Don't call out; _____ your hand.

15. She _____ her head from the pillow when she heard the strange voice.

Practice 2

Write three sentences using some form of **rise** and three using some form of **raise.**

1. _____

2. _____

3. _____

4. _____

5. _____

6. _____

SIT/SET

1. *Sit* **means to seat oneself.**

   ○ The past tense of *sit* is *sat.*
   ○ The past participle of *sit* is *sat*

Examples: *Sit* down.
I *sat* in the soft chair.
I have *sat* here for a whole hour.

2. *Set* **means to place or put someone or something in a place.**

   ○ The past tense of *set* is *set.*
   ○ The past participle of *set* is *set.*

Examples: She *sets* the cigar in the ashtray.
Please *set* the lamp in the corner.
We had *set* them over there, but we moved them later.

Practice 1

1. My Great Dane loves to _____ on the grass.

2. He just _____ there and did nothing.

3. Don't _____ a glass on the edge of the table.

4. You shouldn't have _____ in that chair because it is very unstable.

5. The student _____ the theme on the instructor's table.

6. After the final, _____ on a bench and take a couple of deep breaths.

7. The passengers on the train _____ there and watched the old man being mugged.

8. If you _____ the couch in the middle of the room, you will see the view from the window.

9. Have you _____ the cheese near the bowl of fruit?

10. If you hate to _____ all day, don't become a secretary.

Practice 2

Write three sentences using some form of **sit** and three using some form of **set.**

1. _____

2. _____

3. _____

4. _____

5. _____

6. _____

SUPPOSE/SUPPOSED

1. *Suppose* **means assume, guess, or think.**

Examples: I *suppose* that you are right.
          Do you *suppose* that you will be there later?

   ○ The past tense of *suppose* is *supposed.*

Examples: I *supposed* that you were right.
          He *supposed* that the student would be absent.

2. *Supposed* **means ought to or should. When you mean ought to or should, always used the** *-ed* **ending—***supposed.** *

Examples: Are you *supposed* to be doing that?
I am *supposed* to do my homework now.

Practice   1

1. Do you _____ that you will be on time?

2. You are not _____ to go through a red light.

3. He is _____ to read that book by the end of the week.

4. They _____ that the final would be difficult.

5. What do you _____ they did?

6. The teacher is _____ to ask for questions.

7. I _____ you are leaving now.

8. The travelers were _____ to leave on the 8:00 p.m. bus.

9. Children are not _____ to play with matches.

10. Children are _____ to play with toys.

11. We are _____ to go to school today.

12. Did you _____ that he would show up?

Practice   2

Write three sentences using **suppose** and three using **supposed.**

1. _____

2. _____

3. _____

4. _____

5. _____

6. _____

*See Part G in Chapter 8 for more work on this verb form.

THEN/THAN

1. *Then* implies time, an action taking place at a particular time.

Example: First I am going home, and *then* I am going to eat supper.

2. *Than* is used in a comparison.

Examples: He is taller *than* I.
She is smarter *than* her brother.

Practice   1

1. If she goes, _____ I will go too.

2. Marty sings more _____ he dances.

3. We all went to the park and _____ had lunch.

4. A wise person listens and _____ speaks.

5. My dog is older _____ my cat.

6. Joan walked to the store and _____ went home.

7. She fell asleep earlier _____ I did.

8. We saw Paul and _____ Mary.

9. Jane visited her father and _____ went to see her brother.

10. My teacher is better _____ yours.

11. Where was he supposed to go _____ ?

12. _____ what?

13. They are older _____ I thought.

14. What will you do _____ , if he is bigger _____ you.

15. My brother is taller _____ I.

Practice   2

Write three sentences using **then** and three using **than.**

1. _____

2. _____

3. _____

4. _____

5. _____

6. _____

THEIR/THERE/THEY'RE

1. _Their_ shows ownership.

Examples: I have _their_ coats.
Robert took _their_ tickets by mistake.
Their books are on the table.

2. _There_ **indicates a direction.**

Examples: I saw the flowers over _there_.
The books are not _there_.
She will be _there_ tomorrow.

There **is also a way of introducing a thought.**

Examples: _There_ are no fast ways to get to Queens.
There is no substitute for hard work.
There are three methods for writing footnotes.

3. _They're_ **is a contraction of they + are = they're.**

If you cannot substitute _they are_ **in the sentence,
you cannot use** _they're._

Examples: _They're_ nice people.
They're not the books I ordered.

Practice   1

1. I found my shirt over _____ , by the table.

2. _____ not coming over tonight.

3. Where are _____ new pictures?

4. If _____ here, I'm going home.

5. _____ is a good film playing down the block.

6. I found _____ test papers in the folder.

7. _____ seem to be too many people in the classroom.

8. Don't go _____ alone!

9. _____ not so smart as they think they are.

10. The tutor helped them with _____ homework.

11. _____ is not enough time to correct _____ papers.

12. _____ going to arrive soon with _____ books under _____ arms.

Practice 2

Write three sentences using **their,** three using **there,** and three using **they're.**

1. _____

2. _____

3. _____

4. _____

5. _____

6. _____

7. _____

8. _____

9. _____

THROUGH/THOUGH/THOUGHT

1.   *Through* **means in one side and out the other, or done with.**

Examples: The train sped *through* the tunnel.
              Are you *through* yet?

2.   *Though* **means although or as if.**

Examples: *Though* it is somewhat damp, I like the weather in England.
              It is as *though* I have lived my life before.

3. *Thought* **is the past tense of the verb to think or an idea.**

Examples: I *thought* you weren't coming.
Now that is an interesting *thought.*

Practice   1

1. Whoopee, school is _____ !

2. David _____ a bit and said, "Hmmm."

3. _____ I like apples, they sometimes make me ill.

4. If you _____ about it, you would see that I am right.

5. The piano got stuck as the movers tried to get it _____ the door.

6. It is as _____ you really didn't want to pass the test.

7. He has to get _____ with his term paper by Monday.

8. My pet seal can jump _____ a hoop.

9. Do what you want, _____ I don't agree with you.

10. With work, a _____ can grow into an essay.

11. This door is not very sturdy; I just put my hand right _____ it.

12. Even _____ Ida enjoys mathematics, she enjoys writing more.

13. The ad writers _____ they could sell cigarettes with pictures of happy people kissing and smoking in a field.

14. We saw right _____ their silly games.

15. If you _____ this would be the last sentence, you were right!

Practice   2

Write two sentences using **through,** two using **though,** and two using **thought.**

1. _____

2. _____

3. _____

4. _____

5. _____

6. _____

TO/TOO/TWO

1. *To* indicates a direction towards a destination.

Examples: I am going *to* the movies.
                She went *to* school last year.

         To is used as part of a verb, the infinitive.

Examples: I want *to go* to school this year.
                He tried *to leave* class early.

2. *Too* means also, in addition.

Example: I'm going bowling *too*.

         Too also means exceedingly, very.

Example: He is *too* small to play football.

3. *Two* is the number 2.

Example: There are *two* books on the table.

Practice   1

1. There are _____ many students in this classroom.

2. Where do you plan _____ go this summer?

3. Where are the _____ dollars that were here before?

4. He _____ finds the homework difficult.

5. This room is _____ cold.

6. _____ friends of mine are coming over.

7. I am going _____ do that later.

8. Open your book _____ the right page.

9. The test was _____ easy.

10. He will travel to Europe this summer _____ .

11. The _____ of them walked hand in hand to the bookstore.

12. He's _____ good to be true.

13. They're _____ old for the team.

14. Are you going _____ college this year?

15. _____ what do I owe the pleasure of this visit?

16. I hope _____ leave the city for _____ weeks in the country.

17. Will you come _____ ?

18. He has _____ do everything twice, _____ .

19. She is _____ smart for such a basic course.

20. What do you want _____ do now that it's _____ o'clock?

21. It's _____ late _____ do anything.

22. There are _____ of them outside, _____ the right of the fire hydrant.

23. She is _____ old to wear hot pants.

24. She walked _____ the desk and took _____ papers from it.

25. It's _____ heavy for me _____ lift alone.

Practice 2

Write three sentences using **to,** three using **too,** and three using **two.**

1. _____

2. _____

3. _____

4. _____

5. _____

6. _____

7. _____

8. _____

9. _____

USE/USED

1. *Use* **means to employ or make use of.**

Examples: What do you *use* to tighten that kind of screw?
                 Did you *use* the right typewriter?

○ The past tense of *use* is *used.*

Examples: He *used* the wrong tool.
                 You *used* the right typewriter.

2. *Used* **means accustomed to or was in the habit of.**

Examples: He *used* to walk to school.
                 They *used* to like dancing.

○ When you mean *accustomed to* or *was in the habit of,* always write the
-ed ending—*used.*

Practice 1

1. She _____ to go to the movies often.

2. You must _____ a large hammer for that nail.

3. He is _____ to getting all A's.

4. Never _____ a long word when a short one will do.

5. My mother is not _____ to cooking for large groups of people.

6. What should I _____ for the dusty furniture?

7. He _____ a dust rag.

8. One never gets _____ to taking finals.

9. May I _____ your phonograph?

10. You _____ it last time and broke it.

11. They were not _____ to taking long hikes.

12. Never get _____ to dishonesty in others.

13. He _____ the buzz-saw last week.

14. The workers were _____ to long lunch hours.

15. Don't _____ that until you are sure you know how to.

Practice 2

Write three sentences using **use** and three using **used.**

1. _____

2. _____

3. _____

4. _____

5. _____

6. _____

WEATHER/WHETHER

1. *Weather* **refers to atmospheric conditions.**

Example: The *weather* is very hot today.

2. *Whether* **implies a question.**

Example: I am not sure *whether* or not I should go.

Practice 1

1. I love the _____ when the sun shines.

2. _____ or not you like it, you must find a job.

3. The _____ affects my mood.

4. Tell me _____ you can come to the Easter egg hunt.

5. What dreary _____ !

6. I don't know _____ I should do that.

7. The _____ report is on after the sports.

8. The class will camp out tonight if the _____ permits.

9. When I talk to Dick, I can't tell _____ he is listening or not.

10. I hate the cold _____ of winter.

Practice   2

Write three sentences using **weather** and three using **whether**.

1. _____

2. _____

3. _____

4. _____

5. _____

6. _____

WHERE/WERE/WE'RE

1.   *Where* implies place or location.

Examples: *Where* are you going?
That is *where* I want to be.

2.   *Were* is the past tense of the verb are.

Example: The boys *were* late for the party.

3.   *We're* is a contraction of we + are = we're.

Examples: *We're* too tired to play football.
If *we're* smart, we'll do well.

If you can't substitute *we are* in the sentence, you cannot use *we're*.

Practice   1

1. _____ can I find the library?

2. The students _____ taking a test.

3. Miami Beach is one place _____ I would love to go.

4. You _____ not here when I arrived, were you?

5. _____ ready to leave now.

6. They _____ wrong and you _____ right.

7. The chairs _____ damaged, but I don't know _____ it happened.

8. If _____ going to leave, we had better hurry.

9. _____ are the books that _____ here before?

10. _____ trying to find out _____ they could locate books on ecology.

11. Later _____ walking to Macy's, _____ we plan to buy a stereo.

12. The tutors _____ helpful, but I still don't know _____ we are in class.

13. Miriam and I _____ good friends until we graduated from college. Now

    _____ almost strangers.

14. _____ the best students in this school, _____ it is not easy to be the best.

15. _____ not what we _____ .

Practice 2

Write three sentences using **where**, three using **were**, and three using **we're**.

1. _____

2. _____

3. _____

4. _____

5. _____

6. _____

7. _____

8. _____

9. _____

WHOSE/WHO'S

1. *Whose* implies ownership and possession.

Example: *Whose* book is that?

2. *Who's* is a contraction of who + is or who + has.

Example: *Who's* at the door?

   If you can't substitute *who is* **or** *who has* **in the sentence, you cannot use** *who's.*

Practice   1

1. He is a student _____ always on time.

2. I don't know _____ it is.

3. I met the man _____ written those strange letters to the *Daily News*.

4. _____ going to the movies tonight?

5. I'm not sure _____ tickets those are.

6. _____ automobile is that?

7. " _____ been sleeping in my bed?" the bear inquired.

8. _____ leaving early?

9. It's hard to find a child _____ never bad.

10. He has been trying to find out _____ report this is.

Practice   2

Write three sentences using **whose** and three using **who's.**

1. _____

2. _____

3. _____

4. _____

5. _____

6. _____

YOUR/YOU'RE

1. *Your* is a possessive and shows ownership.

Examples: Is that *your* car?
                Your smile is dazzling.

2. *You're* is a contraction of you + are = you're.

If you cannot use *you are* in the sentence, you cannot use *you're*.

Examples: If *you're* not busy tonight, come to my house.

You're going to have to be more careful, or *you're* going to hurt yourself.

Practice 1

1. Is _____ instructor a man or a woman?

2. I saw _____ brother in the record store.

3. If _____ ready, we can leave for _____ house.

4. This is my share and that is _____ share.

5. I hope you took _____ umbrella.

6. Do you think _____ to blame?

7. You've done a nice job decorating _____ apartment.

8. I can't find _____ present.

9. Drive carefully if _____ tired.

10. _____ essay is very interesting.

11. Help a friend if _____ able.

12. Better take _____ cake from the oven.

13. I like _____ paintings.

14. Since _____ early, why not help me with the cooking?

15. _____ the best friend I have.

16. Put _____ cards on the table.

Practice 2

Write three sentences using **your** and three using **you're.**

1. _____

2. _____

3. _____

4. _____

5. _____

6. _____